Effective Communication Skills For Couples

7 KEY STEPS TO GO FROM CONFLICTS
TO CONNECTIONS IN RELATIONSHIPS, BOND,
BUILD TRUST, BOUNDARIES, ACTIVE LISTENING,
& BIBLICAL CONFLICT RESOLUTION SKILLS

BY T&L. JOHNSON

Contents

Your Free Gift ...

**DEVELOPING INTIMATE
RELATIONSHIPS THROUGH AUTHENTIC CONNECTION**

https://bit.ly/Moreconnected

While It Lasts!

We know Relationships take work. But if you're willing to put in the work, you'll end up with a diamond.

Who is T & L, And Why They Wrote The Book? ...

At ages 19 and 22, with 6 children, Tonya and Lamont Johnson's journey toward building a strong and fulfilling relationship began. They realized that falling in love is the easy part of today's society, but staying in love is the real challenge. Through their firsthand experience, they have become extremely dedicated to helping other couples improve and save their relationships by learning how to communicate with each other properly.

Tonya and Lamont know from experience that not knowing how to communicate properly can break a relationship. However, they focused on the root cause of their conflicts and began to reverse the way they communicated and handled each other's feelings. They knew that they were meant for each other and accepted that no man should be able to tear apart what God put together, even if that man or woman is themselves. They knew that True Love was worth saving.

After more than 17 years of happy marriage, Tonya and Lamont have learned to build an unbreakable bond with God as the foundation. They have developed the keys to a successful relationship, which helped them improve their own relationship to flourish, and any thought of separation is now a thing of the past.

Tonya and Lamont are now Certified Relationship Coaches, and they wrote this book because God put it on their hearts to share with you how their marriage has survived and is still thriving to this day. As the day it first started! They believe they can help a ton of relationships, no matter the age, race, background, or any other factors. They want to see relationships last! With so much going on in the world today, it's easy to get caught up in all the drama and issues, causing a tremendous strain on the way people view, communicate, and value their relationships.

Tonya and Lamont are passionate about sharing their story and knowledge because they know that their guide can help connect the pieces between you and me to equal us. So you can grow a flourishing family!

Introduction ...

Communication in a relationship is like oxygen is to life. Without it, it dies. –Tony A. Gaskins Jr., life coach.

W HERE THERE'S A LACK of trust, there's probably bickering and arguing; where there's a lack of listening and proper daily connections, It always Equals a lack of communication. Over time, this can give rise to resentment and strain the intimacy in a relationship.

Our spiritual health all depends on our emotional health when the heart is feeling good. We open up for better connection!

We might not know everything about you, but we know the disconnect you could be experiencing in your relationship. Trying to figure someone out to make the relationship work is a game nobody wants to play. If we all had our way, the partner we choose would come with a warning label, mind-reading app, or nutrition facts, for that matter (Shut down and won't talk 40%) (Liar 20%) (Possessive 10 %) (can't keep a job 30%) (Laugh Out Loud).

Yeah, that would be nice. But, on a serious note, and unfortunately, relationships or partners don't come with warning labels. Still, fortunately, they do come with warning signs that, if we pay attention when dating or in our relationships, could stop an unhappy marriage or an abusive relationship, amongst other things. But, on the plus side, they may show signs of a keeper, which could be the start of a love story.

For us, a knock on the door sparked our love story. Let us be the first to say we didn't follow the biblical way of doing things like the majority.

Had we done things the right way as God intended, we're sure the in-between time would have gone much smoother.

Our reality was after hooking up, dating, and shacking up, A year into the relationship; we're now expecting a baby! Though we were both genuinely happy about having a baby, we were already blessed with 5, and this would make #6. Still, without hesitation, we decided to make the best of what life had given us. One year and nine months later, on February 14th, we got married. We knew we wanted to set an example of real love for our children, so showing what true love looks like in the home between parents we felt would help them spot artificial love, knowing that this could sometimes be tricky.

The odds that at least 2 of our children (if not all) would one day have a family of their own were high; our mission was to be that model for them that was missing in our lives. This was no easy task!! As the children grew into teens and started their own rebellious stages in life, we began to have more arguments and disagreements.

Being Married with kids will bring it all out!

Learning to keep them on the right track put a wedge in our marriage that we were unprepared for. We disagreed on how the other should handle certain situations and punishments given to the children for their actions.

Meanwhile, as the goals got more significant, A brief sit on the porch became disgusting. To look around at the same people outside doing the same thing they were doing when we left for work and came back from work, not reaching for anything became depressing, causing more stress on the relationship. We were living in public housing; don't get us wrong, we don't knock at all. Living there contributed to our growth in life 100 percent, but we knew we couldn't stay there. The surroundings and atmosphere needed to align with who and what we wanted to become.

We were working hard at a 9-5, stressed and going nowhere fast in our eyes. Ultimately we knew with so much distraction in our lives, we had to be the change we sought for the sake of our marriage. Let the truth be told, nobody ever knows what goes on behind closed doors, and life certainly didn't spare us any hurdles at all, but we had two things constantly on our side helping us fight back;

1. God! We knew that what God put together, no man nor woman Could tear apart, not even ourselves. So keeping God first in our marriage assured us we were grounded on a good foundation.

2. We Started working smarter, not harder, on our issues and ourselves. This included getting closer to God and **personal development daily**, changing our mindset, working on our communication skills, and analyzing other couples in our lives at this time. Taking note of how they were moving in their relationships, why they are no longer together, and why some are still striving.

As time passed and we grew older, things began to change; We purchased our first home and started our own business based on our need to be happy with life and show our kids different from what we saw growing up. So naturally, the older us demanded a different type of attention amongst other things from each other. So we sought new communication skills to get to know the older, wiser versions of each other to better our marriage. As you will learn later in this book, two versions of you might appear in your relationship. Depending on which one shows up in your relationship, you'll have good communication skills or poor ones. The crazy thing is that poor communication was at the core of our relationship. We know if it is not **transformed, it will be transferred.**

Looking back, 20 years together, finding the missing pieces and taking action was the 2nd best decision for our relationship. So Hell Yeah, Relationships get complicated, and yes, at times, you may feel that giving up on yours might seem like the easiest option, but for us, our motto in life and our relationship is N.G.U. (Never Give Up) , We believe true love deserves a fight! Key point TRUE LOVE. Don't get it twisted for one second. We're not telling you to stay anywhere you're being physically or mentally abused, unwanted, or not feeling the love. There is a thin line. You must know the difference and learn it quickly.

It's no secret that social sites are one of the biggest distractions of the modern day. With that said, human nature is to be competitive against one another naturally. But now, with social media at play, being heavily involved in modern-day social media competitions takes things to another level. Also, with the time spent on social media, most have little to no contact with their partner. All contributing factors are where everybody has to be somebody, look a certain way, or project a financial situation that doesn't exist. Just think about it; with so much technology right now, it takes away from just some good ole communication. Most people don't know how or care to sit down and have a face-to-face or even a good talk on the phone.

They'd much rather text or slide into each other's DMs. Sadly these days, people think they know everything about each other in six to eight weeks. Then make an instant decision on whether to stay together for the long haul. The world we are living in keeps advancing at an unprecedented rate. 57.5% of people ages 15 and 20 are unwilling to get associated and form relationships with others in their communities. People thrive on exposing each other rather than maintaining their friendships. Filters and expensive beauty products that don't even work stand behind unrealistic expectations and shallow standards.

Current relationships are challenging enough with social media now at play, and it's much harder for some to keep their trust, communication, and relationship strong. Before we move on, it's important to point out that we trust one another in this modern tech world. There is no accusing or assuming. But we also give no reason for distrust. We share the same social media pages and passwords, everything is open. We do this, so there is no guesswork open book.

If you're married or in a serious relationship, try this along with the seven steps and worksheets we provide later in the book for an even more loving, trusting, lasting relationship or marriage.

We would like to be the first to say Congratulations on being among the few modern-day people favoring a genuine connection with one person over hundreds of "likes" from strangers! Circumstances may vary, but if you've chosen to read this book, We'll help connect the pieces so you, too, can become the power couple you were destined to be, growing and building a healthy relationship rooted in mutual respect, love, and trust.

You will experience the most improvement if both partners are receptive and open-minded. If not, you alone must be the change you want to see and lead by example.

You can't help who you fall for, but you can dictate how well the relationship works. Before we move on, let's address some of your assumptions about us and this book.

"You've been going strong since you got together; You wrote this book to teach others what naturally came to you."

- Well, that is not true at all. Once we noticed that communication was our disconnect and was causing 100% of our disagreements, we decided to save our marriage! We needed help! And to do so, we had some bridging to do in our communication. The main reason we wrote this book is that we see so many people going through the same things as us, letting that break them apart instead of pulling them closer as they did us. We've been through many ups and downs over our 17yrs of marriage, and it took us years to figure out how to better our communication skills to get on the same page and grow together. We're still a work in progress.

It doesn't come naturally or easily. Some days it's still quite challenging. This book results from the best knowledge and skills that served us well for almost two decades.

And it's on our heart to pass it on to you so that you can enjoy open communication & lasting love, trust with boundaries and effectively handle conflicts.

"You must have life all figured out! You've found the secret to always being on the same page and having nothing to fight about."

- No. We did not. We disagree on things, and sometimes emotion runs wild. No one can always be happy. Life happens, but we know how to deal with it and get through it better together. We do not allow things to come between us. We understand where we're headed in life and marriage.

"You're pulling through for the kids, as all parents do."

- No, not at all. The kids are all grown up for the most part. We're empty nesters! After all this time, we are in love, and we would do everything all over again if it meant us feeling this way.

"You will take my hand and fix my relationship for me."

- Nope. Ultimately fixing the relationship is all on you. We will share some valuable skills and resources to open better communication between you and your significant other, but it's still up to you to take action. And be the change you want to see; you'll see the people around you catch on.

"This will be an easy ride, and I'll feel silly for being so upset and dramatic about it."

- Nothing you feel is silly, and this will be challenging. However, the steps we've come up with are simple. Still, they're only simple if you're willing to do what's hard, including being vulnerable, truthful, and listening to your partner even when what they say doesn't please you. You'll also need to learn to trust again—wholeheartedly, in a way that opens you up to pain even more, Yet, trust your partner not to hurt you. It's all or nothing, and relationships take work.

This book shares some essential communication skills, strategies, biblical principles, and other valuable information that works. But here's the thing, you gotta take action and " work " it to get the result. Action is the key to building the life you love together. You have to finish this book! We've also included some **worksheets** and **activities** to get you started on taking more action. If possible, grab your spouse or significant other. Completing the worksheets together is also an excellent way to bond and share.

Most important open up communication and start the transformation process because we don't want it to be transferred to the next generation. Nothing would make us happier than helping you save your relationship or marriage. And to see how this can impact your family. If you can't read the whole book all at once, skim through it, scan the QR code go through the workbooks and worksheets at least.

If you're up for it, this could be the most rewarding experience of your life. It sure was for us.

Worksheet Activity ...

Take some time to complete the worksheet below.
Scan the Qr code or visit the link below.

- Family Patterns Assessment worksheet

http://bit.ly/3YKRdUL

Chapter 1: You're Not Struggling Alone

"You can't see the picture when you're in the frame."— *Les Brown.*

IF WE'RE TALKING ABOUT warning labels that should come with partners, I think a mandatory one should read "WARNING: 100% HUMAN." I'm human, and my spouse is human. I'm stating the obvious but humor me; what does this mean? It means we are flawed and liable to mess up now and then, that we feel hurt and can inflict hurt. It means we can act irrationally or feel things that aren't always rational. It means that we'll both take missteps, and we'll both have our struggles. It's never easy to give your partner or yourself the grace you deserve in this regard, but it's necessary here.

Whenever I pick up a self-help book, I feel like I am at my first therapist's appointment again. We don't want this to be of those for you. For some reason, many people (us included) feel a little shame when asking for help. It's like admitting that you've failed at something you should know how to do, which sucks. There's no shame in needing help; we all need help at some point or another.

Recognizing that you need help can be as challenging as seeking it, so please know it's incredible that you're taking this first step. That you're struggling right now is not a failing on either of your parts; it just means it's time to take the car in for a service. Tune some things up, replace some parts, and maybe throw on a new coat of paint—the exact car you love but upgraded and improved so that it can run for a long, long time.

Next, you must know that you're not alone in your struggles. Any relationship problem you have had or will have, someone else has already been through. Thousands of other couples are experiencing the same things you are right now! It's not insurmountable, and it's not unfixable. Now, we are not just trying to make you feel better. It's just the truth. We've probably been through whatever you're struggling with, and we're still here to tell the tale and guide you through it. Relationships are only sometimes going to be smooth sailing, and that's also perfectly okay. Your relationship is not the only one that goes through rough patches; some patches are rougher than others, but that's just a part.

It's wise to seek advice and help from outside sources rather than both of you repeatedly beating your heads against the same wall. We call that insanity; let us elaborate further and say that seeking help from experienced and educated sources is smart. Help can come from a counselor or support group, books (like this one), podcasts, and re-lationship coaches like ourselves. What matters is that you take steps toward bettering the situation you find yourselves in.

Now, we're here to mainly deal with communication in a relationship and how to improve it. You may not see communication as your main issue. Still, you would be surprised at how much conflict poor commu-nication styles can create.

Take Ralph and Emma, for example. Ralph is thirty, and Emma is twenty-six. Not much of an age gap there, but they do have a commu-nication gap. They have only been together for six months. While he's never found someone more compatible, he's also noticed that Emma needs help expressing herself. They both have barriers to their under-standing of each other. Emma doesn't like emotional conversations or heavy topics. She's also uncomfortable telling him when he's done something that bothers her and engages in passive-aggressive behav-iors rather than being direct about her displeasure.

If Ralph tries to revisit conversations to resolve, they fight before Emma leaves to cool off. Only to return and act like nothing ever hap-pened. He only ever knows that she's upset with him once all her re-sentment has bubbled and she lashes out. So now, Ralph has no idea how to broach any problems he might have in the relationship because he doesn't know how she'll react. He also has no idea how to bring this issue to her because he doesn't know how she'll respond. So how should he approach this situation?

You may be thinking: These two are having a severe breakdown in communication very early in their relationship, which isn't a very promising sign. But the hard truth is, they may still need some growing up to do as individuals. It's good that the truth of who they are and their struggle is coming out early in their relationship.

Humans are constantly growing and will do so for the rest of our lives if we wait until we have it all together to get into a relationship with someone. Then we'll never have any fulfilling relationships. What Ralph and Emma can do is make a commitment to acknowledging their weak points as individuals and as a couple. And work toward growth and solutions in those areas that will allow them to coexist peacefully. This sounds easy, but it can be challenging. It takes dedication and hard work daily.

Since Emma's communication style is conflict-avoidant. It may be hard for them to resolve anything, especially if she refuses to talk and shuts down if she feels pressed.

Sometimes, however, who the conversation is being had with is more of an issue than the conversation itself. This is especially true for people struggling to have hard conversations and express themselves. The root of it stems from a trust issue. In the same way, Ralph doesn't trust Emma to handle any conflict well between them, and Emma may not completely trust him with her emotions and thoughts. She shares when she has allowed herself to get so mad that she can't hold it anymore. Ralph and Emma could find someone they trust to talk to and mediate for them. Someone, like maybe a close friend or even a therapist—may gain some ground in their communication.

Trust issues and communication issues are not always mutually exclusive, though. Sometimes the barrier in a relationship is fear. Jason experienced infidelity at a young age when his dad cheated on his mom. He saw how it could rip two people and even a family apart. So, he decided that if it happened to him, he'd do all he could to hold things together. Infidelity was like a curse to his family name because he did have to endure it.

He was cheated on by his high school sweetheart with his best friend. His college girlfriend was untrue. She left at night while he was asleep in her bed—leaving him in the middle of the night to be with someone else. If that wasn't bad enough, his girlfriend of seven years after that cheated on him too.

Jason is now happily engaged to the love of his life. She has never cheated on him. Although he was open with her and shared his fears because of his past, and she assured him she would never do him that way, it didn't ease his concerns or stop him from displaying signs of trust issues. One day he decides to go through her computer to see if he should be concerned about anything. Of course, there wasn't, but his actions created a distrust in his fiancé that he cannot respect boundaries.

Jason has to find peace with his past, or he is liable to inflict some of the same pains onto his fiancé. At the very least, he might create new cycles of hurt, like Ed. Ed has been living with his pain since he was five.

As a grown man, Ed still suffers from the day his father walked out on him and his mom, leaving them to suffer and struggle. Ed now fears abandonment, so he struggles in intimate relationships. You know what they say: hurt people, hurt people. And that's what Ed does without realization. If his girlfriend doesn't communicate with him for long intervals throughout the day or check in with him, he gets upset and breaks things off. This has been his cycle since relationships became a thing for him. First, he disappears or "abandons" these women, fearing they will do it to him first. Then, instead of recognizing the root of his issue and facing it head-on, he runs.

One day, attending a personal development seminar helped him understand his father didn't abandon him. Maybe he was scared or had abandonment issues he had not yet come to terms with, but it encouraged Ed to end the victim story he had been telling himself for years. It also gave him perspective on how he was now causing the same hurt to the women he dated. He was creating a vicious cycle of victims of abandonment. Sharing the same pain with someone else because of fear and trauma.

The seminar leader helped him to create a different narrative in his mind and to understand the importance of acknowledging and communicating. What he was experiencing, especially with those he was in an intimate relationship with. It was the start of creating a different future for himself than the past he knew of his father—the start of a new man. He could now begin to live his life with intention.

Sometimes initial differences in who we are can create gaps in communication and relationship. Being together as long as we have comes without the quirky irritants. We still engage in baby fights almost daily, but we work together. But over the years, we learned how we talk to each other plays a big part, and when we decide to bring up issues—whether it's in front of the company or not could cause some friction. And while it is true, we should pick our battles wisely. Sometimes it comes down to effective communication and a willingness to compromise and not go for being right. When we say effective communication, we don't just mean talking.

We suggest speaking in a way your partner will be open to, actively listening, and ultimately working together to solve problems.

So you see, relationship and communication barriers can result from issues small or large. Now that you know just how human we can be, let's have a moment of honesty. How many of the above-listed problems have you encountered or even been the creator of your intimate relationships? Do you feel a little less like a failure?

Chapter Summary ...

Chapter Summary

A critical thing to remember is to not be hard on yourself. Your struggles are not new, and you aren't the only one experiencing them. Other people share some of the same struggles as you and your partner. However, it all typically boils down to communication issues. Effective communication is a skill you must learn. If you weren't taught it early, you must seek the necessary help in adulthood to learn it. But before you can work on any communication issues. You first have to recognize and acknowledge that you have them and hopefully get to the root cause to work toward communicating better.

Worksheet Activity ...

PLEASE TAKE TIME TO **reflect and take action by completing the worksheets.**

- Couples Conflict Resolution Worksheet

- Solving Problems Action Plan worksheet

Scan the Qr code or visit the link below before moving to the book's next chapter.

https://bit.ly/ProblemPLAN

https://bit.ly/Conflictworksheet

Chapter 2: The Elephant in the Room

" When there's an elephant in the room, introduce him."— **Randy Pausch.**

H AVE YOU EVER BEEN to a family gathering where when a particular family member walks into a room, other family members just stop conversing and start staring and whispering (With the screw face) Like," what is he doing here?" Then the family member who just walked in the room notices he's been talked about, and just like that, the atmosphere changes—been there! You can feel the resentment in every eye rolled. There's a big fat elephant in the room.

The tension is so thick you can't cut it with a knife. Maybe something happened between family members some years back, and no one ever spoke of it. Still, it didn't stop resentment from bubbling up. The same things can happen in our intimate relationships with our partners. In a relationship, you will likely have your share of tense moments. Light banter, criticism, and occasional quarrels are part of the "couple life." However, if these situations are abnormally high, you should work on figuring out why.

We don't sometimes realize that we are constantly communicating verbally or nonverbally what we don't say matters as much as what we do say and how we say it. Recognizing how we communicate can help us to be more intentional about it. Also, allow us to be more understanding. How we say things affects communication way more than what we say.

Communication is essential to any relationship. Even more so, effective communication is vital. Everyone is different. Our perceptions, understanding, what we receive, and how we speak are all unique to us as individuals. For couples, learning our partner's language is critical to communicating effectively.

Effective communication has so many benefits for a relationship. For one, it helps build the trust needed to allow the relationship and the people in it to grow. You've probably heard the saying, "If you don't have trust, you don't have anything." Unfortunately, there's some truth to this.

Relationships have a purpose. A lack of trust in a relationship slows it. It hinders it from fulfilling its purpose and possibly hinders the people in it. But of course, trust is not earned overnight.

It has to be built. Most times, we don't walk into relationships trusting people. Some of us trust a little easier than others. Still, for the most part, we first have to allow ourselves to get to know someone and understand them before there can be a certain level of trust present.

Effective communication also creates intimacy in a relationship. Where there is open and honest communication, vulnerability, acceptance, and support, there is a bond. When you share yourself, you encourage the other person to do the same and create space for you to grow together. Physical touch doesn't mean a deeper intimacy, but it's a benefit.

You may notice a more profound connection in the bedroom that satisfies you and strengthens your love for each other.

After all, sex is supposed to be an enhancement of your love.

Communicating plainly also keeps you and your partner from figuring out what's on the other person's mind. It also limits misunderstandings and ultimately decreases the number of disagreements that would stem from them.

Communicating effectively with each other takes dedication and daily practice. Since we all come from different backgrounds and have different upbringings, we must remember that how we share is either derived from that or affected by it. Some people may have never been taught to communicate. They may have grown up in a family that valued secrecy over openness. Some people may have been shunned every time they spoke their truth. As a result, they fear opening up or have developed a lack of trust in people to accept them or their communication.

Others may have grown up in a household where communication resembled yelling and arguments over respectful conversation. All of these things can affect people and create communication disconnects in relationships. This problem only goes away once it's fixed.

Communication Problems in Couples

Conflict is not avoidable. Conflict can benefit a relationship if you let it work for you.

Unfortunately, now we have more technology usage, which has only grown more noticeable since the pandemic began. As a result, communicating has become more problematic, especially for people who need to be more intentional about it.

Couples with this technology barrier between them may notice that they are fighting more and talking less. Our phone is our best friend! Having to readjust your communication style takes work. It's also more complicated when people face a crisis and, on top of it, have to face themselves. Individuals have to evaluate themselves and sit with themselves more; this is very unpleasant for some. So, sitting with someone else during this time makes it more complex and irritating. You may find that your partner snaps easily on more minor things or that you disagree more over little matters.

For some, there may be no communication at all. Where disagreements usually lead to arguments, they may lead to a shutdown and a refusal to talk. This can stress any relationship out, the same as constant arguing can. Except now, you are no longer acknowledging that there is conflict but trying to avoid it. Sweeping issues under the rug won't bring a long-lasting solution. It can make matters worse over time. You don't want to find that out the hard way.

Resentment and anger can build up, and everyone knows nothing pretty comes of that. It causes distance between people and can even hurt bonds altogether.

The task of communication is to do it without always leading to an argument. Many arguments stem from one or both persons' desire to be correct. Sometimes it's better to lose the battle to win the war. What we mean by that is that allowing your partner to be right saves the heartache of losing their trust and respect.

Let go of pride and let humility be your leading factor. Other times an argument can stem from horrible listening skills.

The 10-Minute Ritual can help you with this. We all suffered from this a time or two, hearing what we want to hear and not necessarily what is being said. So we listen to respond and do not understand, leading to reacting instead of responding anyway. And our reaction usually comes from a defensive place.

We may want to defend our truth, honor, and case, but it will get us nowhere fast. Instead, it could serve us to take the advice of the Good Book. "A gentle answer turns away wrath, but a **harsh word stirs up anger**." (Proverbs 15:1).

This verse has saved us so dearly over the years. Now it's okay to disagree, but attitude is fire, kill the argument with kindness. A Good Communicator pauses before they speak. Try tapping your leg 3 times or counting to 3 in your head. Whatever it takes, give yourself time to pause. Listen twice but speak once. Relationships gain sturdier ground when both parties are willing to listen twice as much as they speak and gain an understanding by asking questions instead of making assumptions. After all, we have two ears and one mouth for a reason.

Healthy Relationship IQ Test ...

Please take time to complete the worksheet below.

Healthy Relationship IQ Test

Scan the Qr code or visit the link below.

https://bit.ly/RelationshipIQTest

Signs That You Have Communication Issues ...

SIGNS THAT YOU HAVE **Communication Issues**

When there is a breakdown in communication between a couple, you'll notice issues like fighting more and having less meaningful conversations or not talking to each other. When a couple fights more, it breaks down their trust. Eventually, they may lose faith in their ability to communicate correctly with each other, so they'll stop talking altogether. This can cause distance and bring about loneliness and a lack of intimacy. Sometimes, breakdowns in communication this heavy lead the couple to infidelity issues or thinking about breaking up.

There is a process to improve your communication skills; the first step is recognizing your problems. Then, how can you evaluate yourself and see if you're struggling in this area?

First, let's see what communication issues look like.

When there is a conflict, how do you handle it? How we respond to conflict stems from how we handled trauma in the past. And the trauma responses happen naturally, and you react quickly as your body prepares you to handle the issue in front of you. Whether it involves actual, emotional, physical, or perceived harm, these four responses are fight, flight, freeze, and some try to fix the problem.

Do you Fight it and lash out with yelling and backbiting? Do you freeze, shut down and stop talking? Do you take a flight to avoid an issue instead of acknowledging it and working toward a solution? Does working toward a solution make things worse so you don't bother? All of these signal communication issues. So are you a Fighter, Flighter, Freezer, or Fixer upper?

In our romantic relationships, for the most part, this fight-flight-freeze and fix response is an overreaction. You and your partner are a team, and you must quickly repair the disconnect with your partner on an agreed-upon solution. Sometimes you must take the **Customer Service Approach when you need to return the relationship to love. Anyway, just remember!**

"It takes two to argue: One to initiate and the other to take the bait."
· **Barry Demp**

Communication Styles

Don't take the bait. We have always been transparent with each other over the years. Sharing our worlds wasn't the issue. The issue was merging two Dominant Personalities in a peaceful and progressing way. When we didn't see eye-to-eye on a problem, we would argue until we were tired and let the matter rest for a while, with no one winning the argument. Half the time, we didn't know what we were arguing about. Then act as if nothing had happened. But we learned this was like putting a bandage on an unclean wound and could be a recipe for infection later, like Ralph and Emma. So now, when we disagree, we discuss our disagreement and talk it out and try never to go to bed angry. For the most part, we calm down and work out the issue then or if emotions are still high at our 1o minutes daily or weekly meetings.

When it's time we sit down so no one feels intimidated and hear each other out. This doesn't work so well with people with an aggressive communication style. As you will learn later on in the chapter.

Proverbs 15:1 --, "A soft word turns away wrath, but a **harsh word stirs up anger**."

This verse taught us to slow down and not stir up trouble when we respond. Which can either escalate or de-escalate the talk. We learned that active listening changed how we perceived what we heard and responded to said things. It helped us in our discussions. We learned what triggers us, what we should refrain from saying, and what words are helpful. As a result, our communication styles have been progressively better over time.

There are different communication styles. Not all of them are effective or even healthy. Some communication styles are passive-aggressive, aggressive, passive, and assertive.

Assertive communication is what we ultimately want to have in a relationship. It is the healthiest communication style. The other three, not so much. Let's focus on those for a bit.

Passive Communication

The person who uses this style of communication is avoidant. They don't like conflict and are usually scared to speak up or don't know how to. They seem to be the more easy-going, nonchalant people, but they may also be the ones you will see blow up least expectantly. This is because they hold everything in until it boils over and is too hot to hold any longer.

You may never really know what this person is thinking, and it could cause you to be doing life with a stranger. They may be distant even when it doesn't seem to be so.

If you are a passive communicator, you can become more assertive by letting go of your need to please your partner at the expense of your own needs. While it is okay to compromise, and it is okay to cater to and serve your partner, a couple should be equal. No person should be getting all the benefits while one is getting little to nothing in return.

It may sound counterproductive but try telling your partner "No" every once in a while. Think about your needs and find ways to share them with your partner in ways they will receive them. For example, imagine for a moment that you and your partner have spent every weekend together. This weekend, however, you want some alone time. If your partner loves reading, find an article about how taking time apart in a relationship can be beneficial. Send it to them and discuss with them what they have read.

Ease into telling them that you want some alone time this weekend. This is especially helpful if you fear hurting their feelings or think they won't take it well if you come right out and say it. This isn't being passive. It is being assertive yet doing it in a way that is comfortable for you and your partner.

Passive-Aggressive Communication

A passive-aggressive person uses indirect communication. For example, they may joke about something bothering them to put it into the atmosphere. While also making it seem like it's not a big deal, even though it is. With them, "every joke has a little truth in it" is most definitely true.

They may openly express their lack of concern for something they are actually concerned about. They may even say something that doesn't bother them when it does, which will show in their actions. Their nonverbal communication may resemble silent treatment or the cold shoulder. They may deny you sex or even pick a fight with you about a different matter because they don't know how to express their issue with what's bothering them. Passive-aggressive behavior comes off as passive until it becomes aggressive.

If you use passive-aggressive communication to handle conflict, we challenge you to speak your mind; be direct when communicating with your partner. Name what's bothering you but be wary of the emotion that arises. Be open to hearing your partner's view and have an open discussion.

Try not to overthink things too much. This tends to be the reason for passive and passive-aggressive behavior. Yes, it is okay to think before you speak. Giving thought to your speech keeps you from saying something you may regret later on or hurting your partner to damage further. But sometimes, overthinking what you want to say can delay a conversation that needs to be had. It can also give fear a chance to rise, which may lead you to battle the issue alone in your head. Now you have a problem your partner knows nothing about because you need to communicate it so they can tackle it with you correctly.

Aggressive Communication

This communication style is loud and in your face. These people may yell, cuss, and even lay hands on others when faced with conflict. An improper evaluation of their emotions leads them to anger or frustration each time. Aggressive behaviors can even resemble manipulation and control. When fear sets in for this communicator, hardly anything is off the table. They are the forceful ones of the bunch.

If any of these communication styles resemble yours even remotely, we challenge you to find out why. Reaching the root cause of communication issues is the second step to rendering them.

Some communication issues may have started in childhood, some in adulthood. Some may have come from unstable and unsafe emotional and mental environments, while others could result from life experiences over time. For some, we simply needed to be taught what healthy communication looks like. For us... it wasn't modeled. If you can pinpoint what your root cause is, congratulations because you're onto something! You have a better chance of curing the issue if you treat it instead of just the symptoms. In these cases, the symptom is a bad case of unhealthy communication. Once you've worked toward a cure for the sickness, it's easier to rid yourself of the symptoms. And let's say these are symptoms you don't want to live with because they have side effects.

Effects of Poor Communication on Relationships

Let's be honest here. No one wants to be in a relationship where you have to tiptoe around because you are afraid of making too much noise if you feel our drift. But, as humans, we want to be free. We want to live. And if that's not enough, we have the nerve to want to be loved and accepted.

Come on! Who do we think we are to deserve such a thing? (Laugh out loud)

Truthfully, we do deserve it. But obtaining it can be hard when we need to learn how to communicate appropriately. How else can we get across our wants and needs to our partners if not through communication?

We risk being unfulfilled and unhappy in relationships that need open communication. And when two people—or even just one—is either one of those things, you already have a conflict. And if it isn't acknowledged and dealt with, it can ruin a union.

Ineffective communication leads to feeling like there needs to be more support from your partner. Unfortunately, feeling like you don't have the help you need can make you more susceptible to life issues. Because you won't know where to turn or feel you can't turn to anyone for help when needed. As a result, you'll go through life alone, even with someone sharing a bed with you every night. And let us just tell you, this can be the worst kind of loneliness.

You may slowly drift away if you don't feel supported and loved. Your focus on the relationship can then be easily disturbed. Tv and social media don't make it any better. You may romanticize being with someone else because you think they can "treat you better." You may not be in the right mind, which can affect other areas of your life. If this is you, check out a good movie Tyler Perry's Temptation: Confessions Of A Marriage Counselor.

Chapter Summary ...

CHAPTER SUMMARY

Ineffective communication is a slippery slope in intimate relationships. One thing leads to another. When communication breaks, best friends become strangers. The intimacy fades, and you begin arguing more than you have civil conversations, arguing over the most minor things. You might even stop communicating altogether.

Negative emotions arise, and sometimes the outcome is not a pretty one. But the good thing is, the damage does not have to be permanent. It can be undone. You must be willing to work at it. You may think, "I might as well move on if I have to start over anyway." There is a catch to that, though. Modern-day dating is not all it's cracked up to be, even if some things are not meant to go the distance.

On the other hand, You found love once, and you can do it again. Finding the love you desire elsewhere may be challenging because only a few people have the mindset to stick it out through rough times. There are some crazy personalities out there, but if you decide that moving on is something you want to do instead. Let's discuss further some of the things you may encounter.

Workbook and Worksheets ...

PLEASE TAKE TIME TO **reflect by completing the Workbook and Worksheets below in the book.**

- Dealing with Loneliness In Your Marriage

- Barriers to Communication

- How To Resolve Conflict In Your Marriage Workbook

- Healthy Relationship Habits Action Plan

- Handling Verbal and Emotional Abuse from Your Partner

- Talking To Each Other Action Plan worksheet

Scan the Qr code or visit the link before moving to the book's next chapter.

https://bit.ly/withLoneliness

https://bit.ly/BarrierstoCommunication

https://bit.ly/BetterMarriages

https://bit.ly/Relationshiphabits

https://bit.ly/HandlingAbuse

http://bit.ly/3IA1a1H

Chapter 3: The Facets of Modern Dating

"A good relationship is both people bringing to the table; a bad relationship is one person coming to the table with a complete meal and the other with a to-go plate." -TNL.J.

C OMMUNICATION IS NEEDED TO begin a relationship, continue a relationship, and also to end it. However, that is not universally understood and is only sometimes the case. Modern dating has made it easier to discard, avoid, and manipulate people than to communicate honestly with them from the beginning. Whether you're looking to get back into the dating pool or you've been in it for a while, some of the things you may encounter could be similar. Knowing how to navigate them and making sure you're not the one causing unnecessary hurt to others are critical.

Nine terms describe some of the more negative dating habits of modern-day dating. They all signal a communication issue of some sort and warrant different responses. These dating terms include ghosting, zombie-ing, carpeting, breadcrumbing, gaslighting, catch and release, peacocking, mosting, and micro-cheating. Because of these unhealthy dating habits, people are left craving authenticity.

Ghosting

The term ghosting is just what it sounds like. In the dating world, it is when one person disappears on another, and they usually do it without any communication; ghosters don't state they aren't interested or don't want to move forward, and they especially don't give an explanation. It's a cold cut.

Ghosting is hurtful to the ghosted. It leaves the ghosted feeling self-conscious in the most negative way. You'd think something has to be seriously wrong with you to get ghosted, right? Not exactly. The issue rarely lies in the ghosted one but rather with the ghost. They could be afraid of the uncomfortable conversation that goes along with sharing their true feelings, whether negative or positive. They may not know how to express themselves, their needs, or their desires.

They also may not believe they must share their departure with someone if they don't think the relationship is meant for them.

According to Melissa Fabello, a relationship educator, in the article, *So You're A Ghost Guy, Like-To-Disappear Guy,* the reasons for ghosting stem from a disconnect from personal accountability. People who ghost don't understand that leaving someone requires a certain level of responsibility. You cannot make yourself accountable for other people's feelings, but you can be responsible for your actions. You're not required to like or be dear friends with everyone. You're not even required to be honest, but if you would like to be respectful of other people, communicating intentions, interests, or lack thereof, are essential.

The best way to deal with a ghosting situation is to realize that it is not you; it's them. And if you are the one doing the ghosting, take a second to evaluate why you leave without notice. If it boils down to fear, we challenge you to face your fears and communicate. Be intentional about what you do and don't want, and share that with lovers or potential lovers. Be honest about when you are no longer interested in pursuing anything with them or if you only want something casual. You and they will appreciate it so much more.

Zombie-ing

When someone "zombies" another person, they pop back up after dealing with themselves. This means they reappear after they have disappeared. This can be done for many reasons. It's normal to miss someone after you cut things off. We all do—whether it's a friend, family member, or lover. After ghosting you, sometimes a person can reappear in your life if they miss you. Sometimes it could be if they just miss what you did for them or the feelings you gave them. They may even come back around out of sheer boredom. Oh yes, it's common. There is always a chance of getting ghosted again when letting your ghost back into your life. So, whatever the reason for their return, it's important to clarify why someone has reappeared in your life.

It can be hard to resist a zombie if you still have feelings for them; you may not have to. Sometimes a zombie wants a full-on relationship again, a second chance to do better, but even if this is true, there is a sure way to deal with a zombie.

Whether you let them back into your life should be based on whether you feel secure in the reconnection and if they have shown proof of a behavior change. Sometimes, a person can pretend they have changed until they have gotten you where they want you—this is a different form of unhealthy behavior we will discuss later. You must be careful of these manipulative behaviors, so giving the new situation time before making a sure decision is best. If you notice any red flags, believe them.

Set boundaries. The zombie needs to know that you know your worth and aren't susceptible to accepting the same behavior this time. Make them aware that you are putting your emotional needs first. If you're not emotionally, mentally, physically, and spiritually secure enough to know your boundaries, holding off on letting this zombie back into your life is best. Always make decisions with a clear mind—not from loneliness, fear, impatience, etc. After all, you're vulnerable to the same hurt. If they are the person who preys on weaker people, this zombie may know that about you. Don't be someone's holiday dinner partner because you're afraid to eat alone.

Caspering

"Caspering" is the less offensive way of ghosting someone. According to Max Benwell in the article, *Ghosting, Caspering, and Six New Dating Terms, You've Never Heard Of,*
when caspering, "instead of ignoring someone, you're honest about how you feel, and let them down gently before disappearing from their lives" (para 4, line 4).

In *Caspering Is a New Dating Trend That's Worse Than Ghosting,* Sophie Saint Thomas writes that when someone "Caspers" you, they may give mixed signals. At first, they are indirect, and then they are vague. Finally, if they're not interested, they may only pretend to be for a while before deciding to end things. This can be as painful as ghosting because it leads a person on before they are dropped without any real explanation.

Remember that no matter how long or short of time two people have been talking or dating, unhealthy dating habits have negative impacts. So the best thing to do is always communicate directly.

Breadcrumbing ...

Breadcrumbing

You see that handsome Guy in the corner eyeballing you or that fine Woman smiling in your direction from the bar, and you find yourself fantasizing about where it could lead. If only they'd stop with the signals and make the first move.

Showing small signs of interest before the approach is acceptable. Still, when someone constantly hints at their interest in you and never makes it clear through direct communication—if they are never taking the necessary next steps to court you in dating—that's when you should be cautious.

This is called breadcrumbing. It's when someone hints at interest in you and gives you just enough attention for you to be interested back, but breadcrumbers need to fully invest themselves. A "breadcrumber" gives you bits and pieces here and there but never the whole thing. It's almost as if they are baiting you. To put it in simple terms, they are leading you on. They send mixed signals and use manipulative tactics to get you where they want, with no intentions of ever pursuing a lasting relationship with you.

If you enter into a relationship with a breadcrumber, you may find yourself giving more than you get in return. Breadcrumbers may do things like make promises and never follow through on them. They may say nice things to you but never entirely show it in their actions. They may even never be fully present with you when you're together.

Breadcrumbing is mental and emotional abuse. People who do it may or may not realize this, so it's up to the person being breadcrumbed to educate themselves. Understand what breadcrumbing is and look for the signs.

Breadcrumbing can be hurtful, leaving a person confused, incapable, and unworthy of real love. In addition, if you are being breadcrumbed, you may become emotionally unstable. Because of this, it's essential to choose wisely if you'd like to move forward with a relationship with a breadcrumber.

There are ways to deal with a breadcrumber.

First, you have to be firm with them. Set boundaries, communicate clearly and directly, remember what you deserve, and decide whether you want to continue a relationship with them.

You shouldn't take breadcrumbing personally. People who do it have their own issues, and it has nothing to do with the person you are.

However, you don't have to settle for anything less than what you deserve. Should you choose not to continue the relationship, let that be known and be firm about it. Shut down any breadcrumbing attempts that may come about once you disclose your disinterest in moving forward because they will try to reel you back in. They may try getting vulnerable or sharing something personal to make you feel differently about them and wrong about ending things.

They may try to be more communicative for a while and then return to their normal breadcrumbing behavior after they feel they have you where they want you again. Don't fall for it. You don't have to deal with breadcrumbing if you don't want to; either they will decide to treat you right or find their next victim.

Gaslighting

"There you go again. Don't start that. You always blow things out of proportion! And you're wrong most of the time. Things aren't what you claim they are."

Does that sound remotely familiar? Gaslighting is when someone intentionally tries to make you second-guess yourself and what you feel and know. You are belittled and made to feel something is wrong with you, and you need to change to keep them happy. But there is nothing wrong with you. You might be right about how you feel and what you think, and you aren't crazy at all. The person who said those things to you only wants to control you and the narrative and free themselves of any consequences of their behavior.

Gaslighting is even more manipulative than breadcrumbing. If you don't recognize the signs early, you could be healing and recovering from the after-effects of it for a long time. It can diminish your trust in people and in yourself. It can take your sense of self-worth away and cause you not to like yourself much. It can turn you into a people pleaser. Gaslighting has many negative effects. If you question yourself or feel worthless because of what someone else said or did to you, you may already be experiencing it, and it could be time to do something different.

People gaslight for different reasons, some being their need for control or power over another person out of fear of losing them or the relationship if they recognize the power they have as their own individual. Also, they may be afraid of getting found out, so they may lie as a form of gaslighting or trick you into believing that you imagine things. However, gaslighters are clever; even if they don't know that they are doing it, they at least know that they are gaslighting you.

Dealing with a gaslighter takes an equally clever person.

The first recommendation would be to not deal with them at all. To decide whether or not to deal with a gaslighter, you have to know if they are one. Let's get educated on gaslighting a bit, So you're familiar with some signs. And knowledgeable on how to deal with them.

So, what are the signs of gaslighting?

- You question your experience as if you have perceived it wrong or as if what you "know" happened didn't really happen.

- You feel insecure or depleted.

- You feel isolated.

- You're constantly being lied to.

- You can never express or talk about your feelings without an argument.

- You make excuses for your partner for their unhealthy behaviors.

- You are afraid to ask important discovery questions because you need to be corrected.

- You see or hear certain things and are told you didn't.

If you have become a victim of gaslighting, you must take your recovery journey seriously. Be gentle with and kind to yourself. Give yourself a break. You may be tempted to blame yourself unnecessarily, but you cannot take responsibility for someone else's actions. How they treated you had nothing to do with you and everything to do with them. The issue does not lie within you. You don't have to change yourself to fit an image they told you that you were not. And remember, you had no idea they were a gaslighter until you got to know them. Don't blame yourself for not knowing. What happened to you is not your fault. Your healing is your responsibility.

If you are still in a gaslighting situation, evaluate your self-worth and how you view yourself and decide if it is worth continuing a relationship.

Focus on the things you can control, not those you cannot. You cannot change how someone treats you; you can only teach them how to treat you and leave the rest to them. If they are adamant about controlling you, you must do what is best for yourself. It will not be easy, and you have the right to mourn the relationship regardless of what the other person did or did not do to you. Don't let anyone tell you that you shouldn't. Healing requires complete honesty and acknowledgment of where you are to move forward. Although Gaslighting is not easy to overcome, the person who did it to you won't be easy to overcome.

Catch and Release

This dating habit is likened to fishing. Someone spends time looking for a potential lover. Once they find what they have been looking for, they engage in communication that leads to a relationship, and right before it gets too serious, they end things. People with this unhealthy dating habit have commitment issues as well. The idea of a romantic relationship seems lovely, but the reality of it is not necessarily their cup of tea.

This unhealthy dating habit can leave a person feeling confused and lacking closure, as it can happen suddenly without any proper expla-nation. The best course of action when encountering this is to move on. Some of these fishers know their behavior, while others may not. Either way, we don't recommend that you make their problems yours. It has nothing to do with you. There is plenty of other fish in the sea. But if you get a good catch, think about holding onto it.

Peacocking ...

Peacocking

Have you ever seen what a male peacock does when he is trying to get the attention of a potential mate? He shows off his "best" feathers. This is the same in the dating world. Many men and women try hard to make themselves seem more attractive, desirable, and memorable. Peacocking isn't always bad if the one doing it is not going to the extreme or isn't being mean to people they think are not "on their level." Peacocks are honestly naturally beautiful animals. So, if you learn anything from them, consider enhancing your natural beauty.

Be authentic and genuine, regardless of any efforts to wow your love interests.

Peacocking can also be a manipulative tactic, as some people may be prone to use it to trick people into believing that they are someone they are not. However, you may be able to spot a peacock if you pay close attention to its actions and words in different settings. For instance, if you meet someone on a dating site and his bio says that he is fun to be around, but when you two meet up for a date, and he barely has any personality, he may be peacocking to get dates.

Dealing with this dating habit requires you to be alert and mindful.

It is okay to recognize early on and decide on a course of action before moving forward. It's almost like catfishing; someone could lie to you about who they are to get you to like 'em, but if who they really are doesn't fit you, it could be a disaster.

Mosting

We talked about this unhealthy dating habit early on. It can be a bit like peacocking but a little more harmful—even more toxic than ghosting itself. Mosting is when they come on strong early on and really lay it on you. We're talking boatloads of compliments, showering with gifts, or saying, "I love you." Please beware! Relationships have stages and phases, and if a person tries to skip them, they may have an ulterior motive, which might be a not-so-good one.

Some people who "most" are looking for quick fixes. They may be bored and need someone to kick it with more often. If they make you feel good about yourself, you will always want to be around them.

They might wish to love, so they need to love harder, thinking it will get them what they want from you. Maybe they need a place to stay or are just seeking sex and know that they can't get either of these things from you without you being genuinely interested in them, which means pretending to be genuinely interested in you. The thing about "mosters" is that they don't stay.

If they find someone else who can supply their needs, they will leave you alone, sometimes without the slightest explanation. It's the old "most and ghost." Yes, it happens, so guard your hearts. Don't be out there trying to fall in love too soon.

Micro-Cheating

Micro-cheating is that "harmless" stuff you do while in a relationship but don't want your partner to know about. Have you ever sent a message to someone you know you shouldn't be talking to, maybe an ex, and then deleted it so your significant other couldn't see it? This would be cheating—even if the message didn't include inappropriate content. Depending on the boundaries of your relationship, this could be inappropriate. Every relationship is different.

Everyone doesn't agree that something like keeping in touch with an ex is shaky territory. So, if that's not an issue for you, and there is a mutual agreement in your relationship that such things are okay, then you have nothing to worry about. But if it has not been a mutual agreement, then yes, messaging an ex is micro-cheating, and it shows in the decision to delete the messages to keep them secret.

Anything that a person feels they need to hide from their partner, especially when engaging with other people, is walking on the dangerous micro-cheating territory.

Chapter Summary ...

Chapter Summary

Here is the thing: Please pay attention to the red flags that show up. Pay attention to your gut. You can be dealing with any number of these unhealthy dating habits, whether dating for a while or just getting in the dating pool, even if you've tied the knot already. If you educate yourself on these habits, you will be able to recognize when you have grown accustomed to receiving this type of behavior or even dishing it out. Then you can properly analyze how to move forward in your situation. If you have previously experienced these behaviors and want to focus on healthy relationships, understand that it starts with yourself. Get to know yourself, what you want, will, and will not accept, and what you have to offer. Then, learn to communicate these things effectively in a relationship. This is especially important in modern times, as relationships require much more time, attention, and effort to succeed because of all the easy distractions.

Worksheets Activity (For Singles and Couples) ...

PLEASE TAKE TIME TO **complete the worksheet below**. (For Singles and Couples)

- Journaling For Singles worksheet (S)

- Sorting Out Your Values For Couples

- The My Ideal Partner worksheet (S)

- Your Perfect Partner worksheet. (S)

- Identifying-Relationship-Patterns For Couples

-

Scan the Qr code or visit the link below before moving to the book's next chapter.

https://bit.ly/RelationshipPattern

https://bit.ly/MyPerfectPartner

https://bit.ly/Myidealpartner

https://bit.ly/SortingValues

https://bit.ly/Journaling4singles

Chapter 4: Modern-Day Dating

"The meeting of two personalities is like the contact of two chemical substances: if there is any reaction, both are transformed." — **Carl Gustav Jung.**

R ELATIONSHIPS ARE AN ESSENTIAL aspect of life. They are valuable to mental, emotional, and physical health. How well we do relationships has been proven to represent how well we will do life altogether. From childhood, we learn how to Coexist with others, and the quality of relationships also affects us now. Experiencing unhealthy relationships at a young age can have lasting effects on our ability to establish and build healthy relationships in the future. When we become young adults and adults, we may have already taken on bad habits that will take some dedication and hard work to unlearn.

Relationships are not easy, but they are the health of life. According to mentalhealth.org, people who are more connected with others through relationships and community are shown to be happier, healthier, and live longer, more fulfilling lives than those who are not. However, it isn't just the connections that matter. It is the quality of those connections that have a real impact.

In an age of expanding technology, people view relationships as much less meaningful than they were in the past. As loneliness and depression increase, so does the desire to connect face-to-face. Social media outlets are used more as a means to connect, and while this can have its benefits, it isn't all good either—especially in the world of dating. It is much easier to manipulate and be manipulated when maintaining relationships virtually rather than breaking the barriers and connecting on more profound, intimate levels. But people have to change their perspective on relationships and be willing to put in the work. In addition, the definition of a relationship has changed over time.

People today have grown more impatient than ever, thus sometimes considering relationships as a modern-day crisis. But it doesn't have to be this way.

How Does Society Impact Our Relationships

Social relationships are the informal relationships one holds in their life. For example, these include friendships, domestic and monogamous partnerships, and relationships with family, according to The National Library of Medicine. They can also be relationships through community involvement, such as connections through nonprofit organizations, sports teams, and events. You may make social connections at work, but social relationships usually do not include those you must have for professional reasons.

Our social relationships are impacted every day by our lives. Things as simple as working long hours, the inability to properly balance work and social life, and even money issues can impact the quality of our relationships. With inflation on the rise, people are stretching themselves thin. People no longer have time for each other as the value of relationships is declining. However, it has been discovered that these same people are missing out on something pertinent to their prosperity. Hard work and money are not the things that make people prosperous.

Instead, it is healthy relationships that do this. After all, it isn't what you know but who you know, right? But our focus on money and prosperity can make us miss out on this little-known nugget.

Today's society is isolated and lonely, more so than ever before. Neighbors don't know each other, nor do they take the time to get to know each other. Families communicate on Facebook and don't get together anymore and enjoy each other's genuine company. Tablets, phones, and computers replace people. People are becoming more scared to be intimate with one another in person, so they settle for an unreal connection. And that's where a lot of unhealthy dating habits become the norm.

Relationships can make us better individuals, which alone can improve our quality of life. They can be a means of support and even guidance. When we surround ourselves with the right people, it encourages us.

Have you ever heard of a tribe? A tribe, in current culture, refers to a group of people who support and complement you in life and purpose.

It is said that you find your tribe once you find yourself. However, sometimes a tribe comes to you before you know where you're headed. They propel you to that place. That is the beauty of having relationships that are healthy and long-lasting.

Relationships are not only affected by society but can also have lasting effects on society. When people are more prone to community engagement, they reap the benefits of relationships. People become happier, healthier, and wealthier if those relationships are healthy. Moreover, these same people will begin to spread these vibrations across their community, inspiring and encouraging others.

How Relationships Benefit Health

Risks of death, anxiety, depression, stress, obesity, disease, and things of the sort begin to increase in people with low social ties, conversely according to research in the *Journal of Health and Social Behavior* (Umberson & Montez, para. 4).

People who are more socially connected and in healthy relationships may experience various health benefits. This includes behaviorally, psychosocially, and physiologically.

Behavioral benefits come into play because healthy relationships tend to positively impact people. In addition, some people want to become better to better serve others in the relationship, so they may choose better behavioral habits. This can be especially true for spousal relationships. Men and women are hardwired to please one another. Therefore, if something someone is doing does not satisfy the other or causes them harm, they may be more prone to eliminate the behavior.

Healthy relationships bring the support systems people need to develop appropriately from childhood to adulthood, even in adulthood. Feelings of support and a sense of belonging—which are psychosocial benefits—reduce stress and any negative health effects that could stem from its presence.

Psychosocial benefits also include becoming more confident, trusting, and trustworthy and not enduring life's struggles alone. Every area benefits from each other and ripples off like a domino effect. If you have just one healthy, intimate relationship, you may see the benefits in your life over time.

Unhealthy relationships do just the opposite. They actually aren't beneficial and are more detrimental than being without connection.

The Dark Side of Social Relationships …

The Dark Side of Social Relationships

When your mental, emotional, and physical health starts to decline, your money becomes scarce, stress becomes prominent, or life isn't as enjoyable anymore after you have entered a relationship, exit fast! But, unfortunately, the results of such relationships don't get any better.

Unhealthy social relationships are not suitable for anyone. Now here's the thing—everybody needs somebody. So yes, even toxic people need people to believe in and encourage them. That's how they find their healing. The trick is knowing who you are assigned to and who is just a distraction for you. You are meant to bless some people with the presence of your being, and some people just shouldn't get the chance at all. In an era where cutoffs are strong, you must know which.

Engaging with people you are not meant to engage with is a case of life and death. Yes, it gets that real. If people with no social life are dying faster than those with a social life, what do you think is happening to people with an unhealthy social life?

Unhealthy social ties increase stress, and stress is the cause of many health issues the older we get. It also increases depression, regardless of age. We may be more prone to look at the dark side of things if our relationships aren't producing any light in our lives. We may also be more susceptible to unhealthy behaviors such as drug and alcohol abuse, failure to exercise or be active, and unhealthy eating habits. This can result from stress or simply because this is the norm for the people we choose to relate with. You know what they say "Birds of a feather flock together. "

Factors That May Affect Your Relationships

Building healthy relationships takes work; as mentioned before, that work always starts with oneself. If you cannot establish, build, and hold healthy relationships, others may not always be to blame, regardless of what was done or said to you. Sometimes it can be some of our own obstacles in the way just as much as others' issues are. Many factors play a role in how we view and foster relationships.

From our childhood, we are taught how to communicate. We watch our parents and anyone else in our lives and mimic what we see. If our parents don't have healthy communication styles that lead to healthy relationships, we will inevitably mimic that, even if we don't want to.

For example, a child raised in a home where their parents argue, yell, and fight as a means of communication may foster these communication habits because they don't know any other way to communicate. Likewise, a child shunned for expressing their emotions may begin to show signs of anger issues because they aren't being taught how to express their feelings adequately.

Instead, it will come out in the only emotion they can muster up—anger and frustration–which probably comes from their inability to openly share their feelings without being shunned. As a result, they feel unheard and unloved. These feelings can cause unhealthy behaviors.

These unhealthy behaviors can follow a child into adulthood. For example, suppose they don't choose to seek help in healing from their unhealthy relationship with their parents. In that case, they will begin to spread vibrations of unhealthy relationships to others through harmful communications and behaviors–which will cause many of their relationships to end.

Past relationships can also affect how we encounter relationships moving forward. They can determine the lens through which we view relationships. For example, a person who constantly cheated in a past relationship may struggle with trust and find it hard to open up completely moving forward.

Dealing with unhealthy relationships can take a toll on one's self-esteem. We can begin to think that something is wrong with us and question why we can't have lasting and fulfilling relationships. The opposite is true for healthy relationships. They can build self-esteem. In the same way, our relationships with our parents, how we learned to communicate, and past relationships can all positively impact us as well.

When parents foster a healthy environment where children can feel their emotions fully and express them freely, they become adults who aren't afraid of their feelings and can communicate with them openly. These children tend to have lasting relationships. Assertive children turn into strong adults. Assertive adults can be intimate in relationships much more effortlessly than aggressive, passive, or passive-aggressive children.

Other factors outside human control can also affect relationships' health or lack thereof. The pandemic created a nationwide environment where people are forced to learn effective communication or face the ruins of their relationships. The pandemic started stress for everyone, enough to weigh on a relationship. So, if people cannot communicate healthily when facing such obstacles, there will be a lack of support and constant disagreements.

People won't be able to be present for each other, and it could lead to more isolation during a time when community engagement is needed the most. On the other hand, the pandemic has reawakened the realization of how important community is.

Even our different stages of life can affect our relationships. Those friends we make in grade, middle, and high school won't always stay around when we go to college and embark on our lives after that. The friends we make in college may not even still be our friends when we leave. Throughout different stages of our lives, we are tasked with learning who we are and who we are meant to be in those stages. Each step usually calls for a different version of ourselves.

These different versions may or may not fit well with the relationships we have in place, not to mention the various demands that are placed on us in each stage of life. For example, a couple that recently married and has children has a whole new set of needs compared to when they were just dating and had no children. More of their time may be taken up with their children, or they may be working more to provide for their family.

The point is that no matter what happens in life, whether good or bad, it can affect our relationships.

These effects can be lasting, and they can be either healthy or unhealthy. It is always up to us to decide how to allow life's woes to affect us. However, if we can be mindful about establishing and building healthy relationships, we can change the narrative of one unhealthy relationship after another.

How to Promote Healthy Social Relationships

Promoting healthy social relationships can start with simply recognizing and choosing to reach out to the people already in your life. We're not saying to use people as crash dummies, but you can practice building healthy relationships with the people you already know and interact with. You don't have to go out and find new people to connect with unless you want to.

Putting your best foot forward means understanding that relationship-building requires intentionality. You have to be intentional about yourself to be intentional about others. So whether you are shy, scared, fed up, or just don't think that relationships are that important, you can break any barriers by doing some soul-searching and getting to the root causes of any of your relational issues.

First off, you need to have a good bond with yourself. Know your limits, strengths, weaknesses, and areas where you are confident and insecure, and be honest with yourself. Don't run from yourself, but embrace and accept all you are not. This is not only the first step to bonding with yourself but also to love yourself. You benefit from social bonds when you have accepted and have a healthy view of yourself.

Once you can healthily view yourself, you can focus more on the crucial things in relationships. You can be vulnerable, honest, understanding, and helpful and share peace and love. You become an embodiment of something powerful, and the point of relationships is to share a little bit of our spark with others.

Reaching a point where we can be whole and not look for relationships to complete or create us into something more will require patience, focus, and hard work.

There will be some things you'll have to learn and some things you'll have to unlearn. There will be some healing that needs to take place and some growth that needs to occur.

None of it is impossible. Healthy social relationships start with the self and trickle down to anyone involved.

Chapter Summary ...

Chapter Summary

Relationships are affected by many factors, whether they be within ourselves or through the actions of others. Acknowledging what is playing an effectual role in our relationships and being honest about them can help us determine how to move forward in building healthy relationships. Health begins within ourselves, and then we share it with others. It isn't something we can leech off of others. If we don't bring anything valuable to the table in relationships, we should not be expecting to receive anything worthwhile. This isn't to say that sometimes we won't be at our best, but we should always work on ourselves to get back to our best and not become why a relationship is unhealthy.

Relationships are the salt of life. They give life flavor. Healthy relationships increase a person's chances of living longer, more fulfilling, and healthy lives. They also instigate wealth. Who we know can ultimately open doors to our purpose. This means we should refrain from entering relationships to take but to share our spark with others and help benefit the communities we live and work in. Learning to trust one another in this modern world of tech was critical in bridging the gap in our marriage. Current relationships are challenging. With social media now in play, it's much harder for some to keep their communication and relationship strong.

Worksheet Activities ...

Please take time to reflect and take action by completing the worksheets. Reflect on your relationship and discover ways to enhance it.

Reflections On Love Worksheet

Scan the Qr code or visit the link below before moving to the book's next chapter.

https://bit.ly/ReflectionsOfLovee

Chapter 5: Step 1—Healing Your Roots

"Inner Child Work Helps Us Get To The Roots Of The Problem-The Core Wounding- Instead Of Putting A Band-Aid Over The Pain Hoping It Gets Better." -Robert Jackman

QUESTION? DO YOU TRUST yourself? Why or why not? Now think about this one: Do you trust your partner? What about your parents? Do you trust your friends or other family members? Why do we ask this? Because good relationships are built on trust. Yet, trust is one of the biggest struggles that relationships face. Without trust, communication cannot be healthy or present, for that matter.

Lack of Trust can stem from many factors, from how we experienced and encountered relationships as children and young adults to our experiences as adults. For me (T), experiencing childhood molestation made it harder to trust just about anybody. Trust in babysitters, certain family, and friends around my children was certainly out the door. In my relationship, I had to learn to trust myself and not the feelings and thoughts that I wasn't good or deserving enough because of what happened to me as a child to 100 percent trust my husband.

He never gave me a reason not to trust him. I just had to learn to overcome these types of trust issues to have a successful marriage. To Heal Our roots is everything in any kind of relationship and self-perseverance. If we can't heal the root, we can't grow to the degree we deserve to. Think of it as a plant. We all know plants with dead spots or leaves need to be pruned. If not, the whole plant will eventually die! On the plus side, when the dead leaves are cut off or pruned, the plant eventually experiences new growth! That's just the way it is in life. Let go of all things that stunt your growth or can cause you health issues and, in some cases, even death. You don't have to go it alone. Reach out to a therapist. Google can be your best friend throughout the process of getting help. Just search!

Trust and Couples

This one is a big topic. First and Foremost, note that we can't make ourselves trust another person. The other person dictates trust by their actions. What we can control is things like our feelings for a person, but trust has to be earned.

Trust is defined as the security we feel in others. "It is the firm belief in the ability, strength, reliability, and truth of someone or something" (Cherry, 2022, para. 5). Trust issues are created when we do not have that sense of security in others or their abilities to be present and supportive for us.

Trust issues can harm relationships because they keep people from getting close. Without intimacy, relationships suffer dullness and lack authenticity. They keep the people in the relationships from growing; ultimately, the relationships don't evolve either. When a relationship lacks trust, there may be consistent disagreements. Since trust issues prevent a person from being vulnerable and intimate, there will not be much talking out of problems. Instead, there will be a need for more understanding and suspicion about whether what the other person says is true.

Trust issues can also prevent people from seeing things on the bright side. Being more prone to look at the negatives instead of living from a place of gratitude and empathy can create loneliness and isolation. In short, when trust is not present, a relationship is doomed. However, it doesn't have to be. As stated before, Like with anything else, trust can be built. When we discovered this, our relationship took off.

Working at trust may be time-consuming, complex, and especially scary, but your relationships will benefit greatly. One of the first steps to working trust is identifying where trust issues stem. Trust issues can be developed from past relationships and experiences. For example, if a person encounters infidelity from a previous partner, it might be hard to trust the loyalty of future partners.

If a person endured manipulation in the past, it might be hard to trust people's intentions moving forward. If someone experiences rejection many times, they might be skeptical that people will accept them in the future.

According to Kendra Cherry, author and educational consultant, trust issues can also result from attachment styles and the Theory of Development. So, for example, when a child is not nurtured, tended to, and guided in the ways they need to be to develop in these areas during their infancy to 2-year-old stages, it could cause them to build attachment styles that create trust issues later in life. Several things could play a role in a person's inability to trust and not trust.

A struggle with trust can reveal itself in many ways. You may feel a need to control your partner or every situation. You may worry about uninteresting things more often. Trust issues can also reveal themselves through jealousy, an inability to believe what people say, and an inability to get close to people no matter how much you want to.

Going Deeper into the Problem and Solving It After acknowledging your trust issue and recognizing why you may be struggling with trust, be brave enough to talk about your struggle. Talking about your struggle can help others understand you and how you think and create space for your growth and intimacy between you and them. Talking also brings healing. When you can talk through your process, you invite support, and with help, you can think more positively about the issue and the solutions.

Again, Talking to a therapist can assist you in becoming comfortable with talking to friends or relatives. A therapist can give you practical steps to opening up to those in your community. Talking to a therapist can also help you identify underlying issues as to why you find it hard to trust.

Besides discussing what you're struggling with, you can face your fears by actively building trust. Building trust means allowing opportunities to trust people. This can mean letting go of any need to be in control. This may look like accepting help when needed or giving your partner the benefit of the doubt. "There are four general factors to enhancing trust in a close relationship.

They include honesty and integrity, non-defensiveness, understanding, and direct communication" (Editorial Contributors, 2020, para. 19). We will add another one and say that forgiveness is a general and primary factor in rebuilding trust.

An inability to forgive someone for their mistakes (or even yourself) can keep the same victimized story in your head and prevent you from looking at things differently. An inability to look at things from a different perspective–or a wider one shall we say–can limit your understanding and affect every area necessary to rebuilding trust. So, our best advice for rebuilding trust is to work on forgiveness.

Forgiveness is a process.

You will have to be patient with yourself and any other parties involved. You will have to acknowledge the ugly parts, look in the mirror, make changes, and accept what may have happened in the past. It won't come overnight. Understand that even when you decide you have forgiven, saying it out loud doesn't make it complete, and neither will you think it in your mind. Even when you have completed your process to forgiveness, and it has finally arrived, you will still be reminded of what happened and, ultimately, every opportunity to regain that grudge.

Sometimes you will wake up and must decide again that you have forgiven. It can be a never-ending process, but eventually, down the road, the fear that comes along with what happened can begin to lessen. So, face it daily, and don't let it run you. According to Taylor Bennett, senior content strategist at Thriveworks (2022, para. 16), building trust means taking risks.

This includes emotional risks, communication risks, bonding risks, etc. You have to be willing to do what it takes to save, establish, build, and rebuild your relationships.

More importantly, you should be ready to do what it takes to better yourself and have the freedom to live unbound by hurt from the insignificant actions of others. Finally, you should want to be whole and authentic. Living with trust issues prevents that, even if those people like parents, caregivers, and other family members are the ones you feel should have your best interests in mind.

Developing Trust Issues in Childhood

As mentioned, trust issues can develop in childhood. We learn to trust in early childhood, from infancy to toddler age. We know who we can trust, how, with what, and how much we can trust them.

We understand this trust through the ways our parents interact with us. When our parents do not nurture our emotions and encourage proper development at this stage, we have an obscured view of people. Trust issues from childhood trauma are in our belief and actions that we will not be accepted, in trusting too quickly, in being overly protective and not trusting at all, and in the opinion that we have to do everything ourselves.

When overprotective, we cannot trust people with small things, let alone the essential things. We might be overprotective of ourselves, our children, or our spouses.

Being overprotective can push people away instead of drawing them near, and for people with trust issues, this can be strangely comforting as some are afraid of getting too close.

Feelings of being unacceptable develop from being rejected in childhood, whether this was by parents or peers. It causes a trauma that makes confident feelings in oneself almost impossible. This can lead to trusting too easily. A person would want acceptance so badly that they open up too soon, quickly, and much too heavily at the beginning of a relationship. How we experience relationships in our childhood can impact the relationships we engage in our adulthood. Either we can learn to trust along the way or project our trust issues onto others and leave a slew of unhealthy relationships in the wake of our presence.

How People Cope With Unresolved Trauma ...

How People Cope with Unresolved Trauma

More times than not, when we experience trauma, we want to escape the hurt and humiliation caused by it. So instead of facing it, we run and try to hide. But the truth is that we cannot hide from ourselves and outrun the pain.

Instead, we must look it in the face and confidently announce our strength in overcoming it. Otherwise, we become someone we don't know and, deep down, aren't proud of.

Trauma can lead to drug and alcohol abuse. These are both temporary feel-good methods; we can sometimes be lower than before when we come down from whatever high we have. However, prolonging and avoiding our healing can make things worse.

We may find ourselves battling depression or other mental illnesses. It can become hard to sleep, to see something on the bright side, and even harder to truly enjoy life to the fullest because of the unresolved trauma and what we have allowed it to do to us.

Our relationships can be affected by our unresolved trauma. Not only will we lack trust in the human ability to be generally good, but we will project our issues onto others. This can cause constant and unruly disagreement between us and others. We may also need to isolate ourselves from others or shy away from any opportunities to build intimate, lasting relationships. We may even self-sabotage.

" A good man out of the good treasure of **his heart bringeth that which is good**; and an evil man out of the evil treasure of his heart bringeth that which is evil: for of **the abundance of the heart his mouth speaketh**. " Luke 6:45 KJV

You have to win the battle between your heart and mind, control it and cultivate it for our good. If we don't deal with our trauma and trauma-related issues, we allow our trauma to control the narrative of our lives. We give it and the people who hurt us power over our lives. As a result, we become victims instead of overcomers. That causes us to have a victim mindset; with a victim mindset, we talk, act, and think like victims. Because of that, we may never take responsibility for our healing and end up going through life blaming everything and everyone else for where we fall short or where things aren't ideal for us. The thing is, the person who hurt you is not coming back to heal you. You have to take care of that!

Tapping Into The New ...

T APPING INTO THE NEW

You can't transform the old you; you must tap into the new to get new results if you want to change your negative thoughts and emotions and improve your physical and emotional health. We have been doing this recently through EFT Tapping, which may also be a powerful tool for you. It combines acupressure and psychological affirmations to help to transform your thoughts.

And help you cleanse the heart a little bit; EFT Tapping is effective for various issues. It is a quick, easy, and safe technique you can use anywhere.

According to its developer, Gary Craig. Most importantly, this may work for you as well:

- *Increase Self-Acceptance and Self-Esteem*

- *Improve Sleep Quality*

- Decrease Stress and Tension

- Restore Emotional Balance

- Improve Overall Well-being and Quality of Life.

However, working with a qualified EFT practitioner or learning the technique from a reputable source is essential to ensure proper application and effectiveness. With practice and consistency, EFT tapping can help transform negative emotions and beliefs and restore overall emotional and physical well-being.

So Let's show you how to do it. Start by saying, "Even though I have this (insert emotional focus here), I deeply and completely accept myself, and It won't stop me."

Now rate the intensity of that emotion or feeling on a scale from 0 to 10, with 10 being the highest intensity.

Next, tapping on these acupuncture or acupressure points:

1. Start by tapping on the side of your hand, the "karate chop point," while you say the following phrase three times: "Even though I have this (insert emotional focus here), I deeply and completely accept myself."

2. On the top of your head: Tap with your fingertips on the crown of your head while saying a reminder phrase, such as "I fear speaking up for myself."

3. On the inside of your eyebrows: Tap with your fingertips on the inside of your eyebrows, near the bridge of your nose, while saying your reminder phrase.

4. On the outside of your eyebrows: Tap with your fingertips on the outside of your eyebrows, along the edge of your forehead, while saying your reminder phrase.

5. Under the eyes: Tap with your fingertips under your eyes, on the bone under your eye sockets, while saying your reminder phrase.

6. Under the nose: Tap your fingertips under your nose, between your nostrils, while saying your reminder phrase.

7. On the chin: Tap with your fingertips on your chin, in the crease between your lower lip and your chin, while saying your reminder phrase.

8. On the collarbone: Tap with your fingertips on the bone just below your collarbone while saying your reminder phrase.

9. Under the arm: Tap about 4 inches below your armpit with your fingertips while saying your reminder phrase.

10. Finally, return to the top of your head and tap for one last time while saying your reminder phrase.

11. After completing the sequence, take three deep breaths and check in with your emotional focus again. Then, re-rate it on the same scale from 0 to 10

12. If your intensity level has yet to decrease, repeat the sequence as many times as necessary while adjusting the phrase and focus as needed.

Many of us, have a lot of heart cleansing to do, so find " your pace " and keep it consistent. **Remember, practice and consistency is the key to moving the needle of life.** Practice and consistency is the key to moving the needle of life**!**

Please Visit The Link Below For 5 Important Video On Healing And More Resources For Tapping

https://bit.ly/HealingYouself

Importance of Self-Care for Trauma Survivors and Their Partners

When you have experienced trauma, it is imperative to take care of yourself. You may only experience the health and growth you need with loving care. Your healing is your responsibility. You have to be willing to stand up for yourself and take back your power. You aren't a victim; you are an overcomer. God's word reminds you that you are more than a conqueror through Him (Romans 8:37), regardless of what you have been through.

Sometimes, we can disregard the importance of placing God in our relationships. We ignore the importance of letting Him steer the boat, a recipe for greater disaster. God wants us to live abundant lives with fulfilling relationships. We have all been placed here on this Earth together because we are meant to commune with one another. Relationships are kingdom wealth, amongst other things. So, if God wants us to have healthy relationships, how much more do you think He wants us to be healthy ourselves? He is a healer, and when we look to Him for our healing, not only do we become whole, but we become new. Everything that affected us in the past becomes like rubble in our hands, and we can finally let it go because "He trades us His beauty for our ashes" (Isaiah 61:3).

Healing takes some time. It could take a lifetime. But it doesn't take a lifetime for you to be intentional about moving toward that healing. Be intentional about what thoughts you give your mind to; control your emotions; don't let them control you. Be intentional about being authentic in every encounter in your life. It won't be easy, but it will always be worth it. And we know you can do it.

With healing comes the need to be honest about where you are with those around you. Give people a chance to understand you and be a support system for you, especially your partner. To love you correctly, your partner must know what being and feeling loved means to you. So, you have to share that with them. That means being honest about the ugly parts as well as the beautiful parts. While it can be hard to talk about traumas, this is where trust is essential. Learning to let down your guard and lean on your partner not only creates intimacy between you and your partner but also allows you to evolve.

There is something called a "couple bubble." A couple bubbles consist of you and your partner. The basis is determining how well you two will show up for each other in your everyday lives and face trials and tribulations. The health of the couple bubble is determined by you and your partner and your communication with one another. Your couple's bubble should evolve as you, your partner, and your relationship grow. What each person brings to the bubble should be equal in significance to each other; otherwise, the couple's bubble is not sacred and secure enough.

A couple bubble for a trauma survivor allows their partner to understand who they are, how they got to a certain point in their lives, and how they are expected to be supported throughout the journey to healing and life. A couple bubble is a way to care for your relationship, partner, and yourself. There are other ways to take care of yourself as well.

Some other ways to begin taking care of yourself would be to engage in activities that make you laugh. Of course, we mean those gut-wrenching, crying-out-loud laughs. Laughter is good for the soul. The more you do it, the less bruised your soul feels. It helps take the focus off the negative and place it on the positive things, even if only for a little while.

Another way to take care of yourself is to spend quality time with your partner and others in your support group who want the best for you and desire to see you better. Continuing to connect with people who love you creates feelings of love and security that you can learn to reciprocate as your trust in the people in your support group grows. You also want to make sure to spend some time alone. When you have gone through trauma, it can be tempting to surround yourself with people all the time to escape the thoughts that come with being alone, but remember that being alone does not have to mean being lonely. Some of the ideas you encounter when alone just reveal the areas you still need to heal and to heal, you have to be willing to do the ugly work that comes with it.

Seeing a therapist is a great route to take as well. Talking about things helps free you from them because it takes away their power over you. Sometimes we think that being silent about something makes us stronger, but if we cannot talk about something, it has more control over us than we would like to believe. So, talk about it.

Visit a therapist personally or allow your partner to come along for support. Either way, I can't express it enough, a therapist can help you work through the issue of your trauma, and that's what you want to do so that you can show up for yourself and in your relationships entirely and without reservation. Seeing a therapist could also help with your communication as a couple. They can be the mediator between you two on your journey to understanding one another. Once you know one another, you can learn how to approach and share.

Tips for Communication

Learning to communicate with your partner through your healing journey can be a rollercoaster ride. Sometimes you may feel confident in what you should say and how to say it; other times, you may need more confidence. However, you don't have to be ashamed of the process that comes with learning to communicate effectively after a traumatic experience. Please understand that you are not alone or the only one struggling. Your partner is your support, so allow them to be.

There will be times when trying to communicate that'll lead to disagreements. To avoid a heightened conflict or to calm one down, take a step back and reevaluate the situation. Assess yourself and decide if you are clear-headed enough to proceed with the conversation. If not, it is okay to walk away to clear your mind and think about a better way to continue the conversation.

Knowing your triggers in a disagreement are also a way to keep it from escalating. Find ways to say what needs to be told without triggering the other person. If one is triggered, being quick to make it right can show your partner that you are invested in the growth and evolution of your relationship and willing to work through any issues to see your relationship stand. Being triggered is normal; however, it should not be intentional. There should be no hitting below the belt during disagreements. Instead, consider your partner's thoughts and feelings at all times. Mindfulness helps you hold each other accountable for your actions and words.

When communicating, a big thing many of us miss is how important it is to listen first. We should always approach a conversation with the mindset of gaining an understanding rather than only being understood.

We should reach a solution acceptable to both parties and not favor one side more. We should refrain from listening with the intent to respond. This is a mistake we have all made at least once. We are so eager to get our point across that we look for more opportunities to prove it throughout the conversation. This usually escalates any disagreements. Active listening is imperative.

You can show your partner that you are actively listening to them by looking at them when they talk to you and making eye contact when possible. In addition, you can repeat what they said to you to ensure you have heard them correctly. This also helps you to register what you heard and, before responding, ask any questions if you don't understand.

Developing healthy communication skills takes practice. Only some people know how to communicate healthily; there's nothing wrong with that. It took us a while. As long as you are open and willing to learn, you can master communication in any relationship. Accept that there is a process, be patient with yourself and your partner, and work toward it together. Two heads are always better than one. When you struggle, the other can help, and vice versa.

You can remind each other when things are flying off the handle and bring each other back down to Earth. Invest in the process and watch as you yield the fruits of your labor.

Rebuilding Trust in Your Relationship

Whether your trust was broken or you broke someone else's trust, there comes a time when you have to decide that enough is enough and choose to trust again. Trust has to be rebuilt after it has been broken. This can be harder than the initial building of trust sometimes but know that trusting again—yourself and others—is not impossible, and there is hope for you. So, what does it take to rebuild trust?

As we discussed before, trusting again requires you to be willing to take that risk. Relationships are risky. Trusting is risky. Trust has to be a foundation for a relationship, though. Trust is necessary, for without it, there practically to be a relationship. At least the value of it goes down tremendously. That's like a house whose foundation is unlevel or whose roof is fragile.

Until the problem is fixed, there is always a possibility of the house collapsing. So let's take practical steps to improve your trust issue.

Think about why and how your trust was broken. Understanding why something happened can help you feel confident, knowing it won't happen again if you have expressed your hurt to your partner and set expectations for them for the future. Then, not only does your partner know what to do in the situation, but you have also given them a chance to redeem themselves, which can go a long way.

Setting boundaries is also foundational in rebuilding trust. Express what is and isn't acceptable, and allow your partner to do the same. Don't overstep any boundaries. Be considerate of your partner just as you want them to be to you. When you are both openly and equally putting in effort in the relationship, it builds confidence and removes any reservations that may be present. This brings us to our next point. Work on your self-esteem.

Sometimes not trusting your partner boils down to a lack of self-esteem. Self-esteem can take a hit when something is done to break trust. It can also result from some other incident that happened in the past. To build self-esteem, invest in yourself. Take time to do what you love, pamper yourself, and encourage yourself. Read self-help books, go to a therapist, and write in a journal. Just be sure to have some fun. When you have healthy self-esteem, you handle issues healthily.

Rebuilding trust requires communication. Talk to each other. Share how you feel and why. Share big and small things. Also, Be open and vulnerable with one another. The more you do it, the more it becomes a habit; before you know it, you are again comfortable with your partner.

Understand that you agree to trust again when you decide to remain in a relationship after breaking the trust. So, it is best to talk through any issues that caused trust to be damaged or resulted from it and move forward. Refrain from dwelling on the past. Instead, live in the moment and work toward the future.

Remember what happened in the past so you'll remember to avoid making the same mistakes as a couple, but don't live there. Don't use the past as ammunition in arguments. Don't use the past as a reason to mistreat your partner disrespectfully or without remorse.

Understand your partner has broken trust; they probably hurt behind it as much as you do and desire just as much to regain your trust and to trust themselves again.

While we're on the topic of trusting ourselves again, there are steps that you can take to regain your partner's trust if you have broken it and, therefore, your own trust. The number one thing to remember is patience. It can be tempting to want the trust to happen immediately, especially if having it will soothe any hurt you feel behind breaking it in the first place. However, rebuilding trust does not happen overnight. It is a process, and you can't skip it.

First off, learn to trust yourself again. You are human, and you are allowed to make mistakes. Be intentional about growing through your mistakes and not repeating the same ones. Communicate your expectations with your partner about your need for a chance to grow from the mistake. Communicate that you do not expect to have your mistake held over your head, and express how you feel about your error. Share what you plan to do to move forward. Remember to support your partner in their journey to trust you again. Also, be that support for yourself. We tend to be harder on ourselves than others. Cut yourself some slack and love yourself. Free yourself from the need to be perfect and get it all right at once. Take steps toward your healing as well.

Chapter Summary ...

CHAPTER **S**UMMARY

Trust is an essential aspect of every romantic or platonic relationship. Without trust, it is hard to have a bond fulfilled with intimacy. It is hard to have a healthy relationship. Insecurities and other personal issues will block the path to a healthy relationship. Until those issues are worked out, every relationship a person with trust issues tries to enter will only go so far before it eventually ends.

You cannot control what was done to you, but you can have a say in how it affects your future. Take the necessary steps to heal to be your best self, and share that version of yourself with others. Embrace where your trust issues began. What happened in your life to cause you to have problems trusting others? How can you reverse the damage so you can live a fulfilling life? You don't have to live broken; you can be whole. Whole people create fulfilling relationships.

Worksheet Activities ...

Please take time to complete the worksheet below., if it fits.

If not, just complete the last three.

- Overcoming Infidelity Checklist.

- Reviving Your Relationship After Infidelity worksheet

- Bringing Back The Joy In Your Marriage

- Increasing Loving Communication With Your Partner

- Manage The Rough Spots And Keep Your Marriage Together

Scan the Qr code or visit the link below in the book before moving to the book's next chapter.

https://bit.ly/RoughSpots

bit.ly/IncreasingLoving

https://bit.ly/ThebackJoy

bit.ly/REVIVING

bit.ly/INFIDELITYCHECKLIST

Chapter 6: Step 2—Healthy Boundaries, Healthy Relationships

" To Find Your Balance In Life And Relationships Is To Create Healthy Boundaries." -TNL.J

E VERY HEALTHY RELATIONSHIP HAS healthy boundaries. Boundaries are put in place to protect both parties' emotional, mental, physical, and spiritual well-being. Protecting boundaries builds trust and intimacy, whereas overstepping boundaries can do the opposite.

One of the most essential boundaries we have in place is that our money is OUR money, and our accounts are OUR accounts. The outcome is that we have zero fights about money, who spent this, who's buying that etc. What's ours is ours. We've seen couples split from just that type of division. Setting boundaries does not equate to building a wall between you and your partner.

People with healthy boundaries generally have a positive outlook on themselves, and when these boundaries are established in a relationship, they allow the same positive outlook for their partners. With clearly established limits, it is easier to know what is and isn't acceptable and where to draw the line on some things.

It's hard to see where you stand with your partner, what will draw you closer, and what will tear you apart. Unclear boundaries can also cause unhealthy and confusing communication.

Setting Boundaries

"Setting boundaries is a way of caring for myself. It doesn't make me mean, selfish, or uncaring (just) because I don't do things your way. I care about me, too" (Kozlowski, 2019, para. 3). Boundaries establish the way you want people to treat you. They set expectations for others, and, in a way, you share who you are and are not. Boundaries keep you from being mistreated, manipulated, shamed, and left uncomfortable. Healthy boundaries also keep us from being taken advantage of, overextending ourselves, and being unhappy with ourselves.

Setting healthy boundaries looks like you speaking up for yourself and sharing with others what is and isn't acceptable according to your beliefs, past experiences, and morals.

Healthy boundaries have consequences when they are crossed. They are upheld by the one establishing them just as much as they want those around them to support them. If we don't hold to our boundaries, it becomes hard to expect others to. Setting healthy boundaries shows the respect we have for ourselves.

It is perfectly normal for us to want to please our partners. However, our livelihood should not revolve around pleasing them so much that we abandon ourselves. Not setting healthy boundaries usually stems from a fear—the same fear that causes us to be people pleasers. We fear that our partners will be upset, that maybe they will abandon us, or perhaps it will cause an argument. That is why setting boundaries should be something we do when we first meet and establish a relationship with someone. We tell people how to treat us from the start.

However, we cannot force them to adhere to our boundaries; we can only decide the course of action if they don't. Remember, if someone does not respect your boundaries, they do not respect you.

Setting healthy boundaries helps you be assertive and confident and have more time for what you genuinely enjoy. You can care for yourself and therefore show up better in your relationship. Setting healthy boundaries builds confidence in oneself and your partner and grows your trust in each other. Boundaries are important.

To set healthy boundaries, you have to know your limits. Your limits tell you when to shut it off. They aren't anything to be ashamed of, and boundaries help you to embrace those limits. So what kind of boundaries can you set for others? You can set mental, emotional, spiritual, material, and physical boundaries.

Mental Boundaries

You can set mental boundaries with yourself and with others. You get to choose the thoughts you allow into your mind. You can also choose what you watch or listen to that may affect those thoughts. You can choose if or how you share your thoughts with others and who you share them with.

If every time you share your views and opinions with someone and they have something negative to say, or they make you feel worthless, or as if your thoughts and ideas don't matter, you don't have to share with them. Set a boundary to only share with people who show value in your thoughts.

Emotional Boundaries

Permit yourself to feel your emotions to the fullest and let no one have the power to take that away from you. That is the start of setting healthy emotional boundaries. You are responsible for your emotions and no one else's. You are also not responsible for anyone else's emotions. When you have healthy emotional boundaries, you understand that happiness is an inside job. When you have healthy emotional boundaries, you express your feelings and do so in a healthy way. Your emotional space is reserved for things that matter to you when you have emotional boundaries.

Spiritual Boundaries

With spiritual boundaries, you hold fast to your morals and beliefs. You don't allow others to impose their spiritual views on you, and you don't do it to others. You protect your spirit in whatever ways you deem necessary. Spiritual boundaries promote spiritual health and wellness. Without them, you risk going against your beliefs and putting yourself in uncomfortable and compromising positions.

Having spiritual boundaries can look like you refuse to engage in activities against your beliefs. It can also involve engaging in activities that support your spiritual beliefs. It can look like choosing to take some time away from others to dedicate to prayer and Bible study. Keeping Sundays sacred for fellowship and worship can look like keeping Sundays holy. Whatever spiritual boundaries are to you, it is crucial to hold yourself accountable. No one else is responsible for your spiritual health.

Material Boundaries

Material boundaries are set with your possessions. You decide what is and is not acceptable regarding the things you own. For example, if you choose not to allow eating in your car, you will set that expectation for anyone who rides in your vehicle. How you choose to set boundaries and what you decide to place them on is your choice. You do not have to explain it to anyone, and you do not have to compromise it for anyone, either.

An example of not compromising your material boundaries would be telling someone no when they ask to borrow money and that you have already spent everything within your budget. You don't have to share your business with them; you would simply let them know you don't have it.

There are many benefits to setting boundaries. First, boundaries determine your health and wellness. If you set healthy boundaries, they will show as much as if you don't set them.

When you say no to things you don't want, you make time and space for what you want.

Unfortunately, it can be hard to say no, especially if you are a people pleaser. People pleasing can make you lose a sense of your self-worth and lead you to do things that are ultimately against who you are at the core. That's why sticking to your boundaries is essential.

Your mental, emotional, spiritual, and physical health is impacted when you set healthy boundaries. You become more responsible for yourself and act with an understanding that others are also responsible for themselves. You don't take on the unnecessary baggage of others or allow their emotions to affect you. You don't let their thoughts become your thoughts. You don't allow their beliefs to make you question what you believe. You don't give in to their demands to make them feel better, especially if you know their demands are unsuitable. Your boundaries help you to love yourself and others more.

You will find that when you set healthy boundaries, you don't experience as much depression. You get to change your narrative from a sad one to one of joy because you're investing more into yourself. Setting boundaries doesn't mean being selfish. It is an understanding that you cannot give what you don't have. So, you decide to pour into yourself first so that you can pour into others. If you are not well, you are no good to other people.

Healthy boundaries build confidence. You begin to trust your ability to make good decisions for yourself, your well-being, and your life path. You become more satisfied with who you are and where you are in life. Fewer things can negatively impact your worldview. How you view things becomes filtered through a lens of love and grace. Surprisingly enough, when you set healthy boundaries, you are more compassionate, empathetic, and understanding toward others. You also become more confident about asking for what you need. You're assertive in your speech and don't feel the need to veer toward aggression to get what you want. You're honest and open, your integrity grows, and you become more authentic.

Your finances are positively impacted by setting healthy boundaries. Money can be when you set healthy boundaries, your issue if we allow it to be. Allowing people to use you monetarily can stress your finances and life altogether. Setting budgets and telling people no when you don't have extra money to lend is necessary. Don't allow people to make you feel bad for saying no or not having it. These are ways to set monetary boundaries and see positive results. You work hard for your money, and how you spend it is your choice. It is the responsibility of others to work hard and take care of themselves. There's nothing wrong with lending a hand if they need it and you want to, but you shouldn't feel compelled or coerced into doing it. It is a choice.

Healthy boundaries can make you feel safe and secure in your own being and relationships with others. As you allow people to respect your boundaries, you start to see who cares about you, who is for you, and who is not. Then you can make better decisions on how to move forward in relationships with others. Healthy boundaries build healthy relationship bonds. People know what they can and cannot do to and with you. They understand where you stand on practical issues and what your worldview is.

They begin to see you for who you are and not what they can get out of you. You become less of someone others can use and more of someone they can connect with. Remember that setting healthy boundaries doesn't make you selfish and will not ruin relationships that are meant for you—or are well within the limits of your boundaries. If people cannot respect your boundaries, it may not be worth pursuing anything with them.

Building The Fence ...

Building The Fence

You don't have to be reclusive to set healthy boundaries. Healthy boundaries don't isolate you from others; it brings you closer to them. Your goal shouldn't be to build a wall but a fence instead. A wall separates, with no possibility of a union, whereas a fence has a gate that opens and closes. Things can get in and out of a fence, whereas with a wall, they cannot. Setting healthy boundaries just means setting the intensity of your pain level tolerance and working toward easing the pains already there.

You can set healthy boundaries by learning to say no. This is one of the hardest things to do, especially with people you love. The risk of not saying no to things you don't enjoy or overstepping your boundaries means overextending yourself, experiencing burnout, and resenting others. "No" is a complete sentence.

You don't have to explain your no or make the blow soft for others to be able to swallow. Stand on your no, and those who love you will accept it.

This doesn't mean you shouldn't be accountable when your "no" hurts someone. An example would be if someone asks you to stop doing something because it causes emotional pain, and your response is "no" because you feel like what they're asking you to stop doing constitutes who you are. However, you must step back and see if a compromise can benefit you.

On the other hand, something you are doing brings someone else emotional pain while they are responsible for their emotions. In that case, you are responsible for your actions and still have to consider how your actions affect others.

Hold yourself to the same standard you hold others to. If you do not respect your boundaries, you cannot expect others to. Don't give in to distractions or pressures of the world and lose sight of what's important to you.

Stand on who you are, and those meant to be in your life will always accept you for who you are. They will love and respect you even if your boundaries make you nonconforming and unique, as you should be.

This goes along with keeping your word. If you say you're going to do something or that you will not do something, hold to it.

Going back on your word gives the impression that you don't take what you say seriously enough, so others won't either. This shows them that they can overstep your boundaries. You do it, so why can't they, right? People will usually follow your lead when learning how to treat you. Be a good example to them.

You also have to be more open and communicative to set healthy boundaries. If you cannot be assertive in sharing your boundaries, you might be overstepped more than you'd like them to be. Boundaries need to be clarified from the start. They're an invisible line that isn't drawn in the same spot for everyone. What may be a boundary to you may not be to someone else, so you must make your boundaries clear. This is done with good communication.

You have to listen as well as, if not better than, you speak when communicating. You don't have to be judgmental in setting boundaries, however. If you don't like something and someone else does, you don't have to turn your nose up at them. Instead, be kind and accepting because that's how you want people to treat you. What you put into the world will come full circle to you, so treat people with respect. Don't assume that you know someone or what they're thinking. Always ask questions to gain an understanding first. Then take the initiative to believe them when they tell you. Allow what you gather from their responses to be your determining factor, not your perceptions, assumptions, and disbeliefs.

When you set boundaries, you also have to be willing to accept that others have limitations too, and you have to respect them if you want a fulfilling relationship with them. Relationships are not one-sided. If they are, they have ventured toward the unhealthy side and need some TLC. If tending to the relationship and trying to make necessary changes does not work, it could be time to walk away. You must know the time for each.

You don't want to find yourself giving too much to something that isn't worth it in the end, but you also don't want to walk away prematurely before giving the relationship a chance to grow. Wisdom and patience are necessities.

Chapter Summary ...

CHAPTER SUMMARY

Healthy boundaries determine your health, which determines your relationships' health. If you are not healthy, your relationships take a hit. Learning to set healthy boundaries can take practice, but it is a skill that can be acquired.

Setting healthy boundaries requires listening to your body and paying attention to your thoughts and emotions in different situations with different people. It requires you to evaluate yourself and your relationships' health to determine what is worth setting a boundary on and how. It also requires you to know what is valuable to you and what you are not willing to compromise on. Another thing we know from experience is that setting healthy boundaries can be especially hard to do when it comes to children. We must be mindful. Depending on the circumstances, we could be hurting them rather than helping them. That's a book in itself!

Healthy boundaries start with you respecting yourself and being an example to others on how to treat you by treating yourself and others the way you want to be treated. One of the most complex ways to set boundaries is by simply saying "no." It sounds mean and ugly, but it can produce a lot of good. It creates space for what is important to you.. and removes everything that is only a distraction or taking up precious time. So when someone or something infringes on your boundaries, you can say "no," and we encourage you to.

Be Assertive and Courteous.

Your "no" doesn't have to be aggressive, and you don't have to be passive with it. Instead, speak compassionately and kindly with a calm tone. Don't be snappy or judgmental in your response. This will serve you well!

Understand People's Tactics

Saying yes can be easy to do with someone, especially convincing. Know the signs of manipulation and be ready when you see them. Remember your boundaries. You are not responsible for anyone but yourself. Saying no does not make you a bad person. It does not mean that you don't care. Shut down any manipulation when you see it by not responding to it. Calling someone on their manipulative tactics could cause them to try harder and cause arguments and stress.

Set Boundaries

Be willing to accept your limits and share those limits with others. Embrace the part of you that says enough is enough, and be ready to nourish that part of you as much as possible. Having limits does not make you weak. It makes you human. Be intentional about not overextending yourself in any way.

Worksheet Activities ...

Please take time to complete the worksheet below.

- Healthy Boundaries Assessment Worksheet

- Healthy Relationship Boundaries - Worksheet

- Dealing With Your Spouse's Untidiness

Scan the Qr code or visit the link below before moving to the book's next chapter.

https://bit.ly/HealthBAssessment

https://bit.ly/1HealthyRelationships

https://bit.ly/untidiness

Chapter 7: Step 3—Using the Power of Two Letters

"It's only by saying NO that you can concentrate on the things that are really important." – **Steve Jobs**

S AYING "NO" IS THE beginning of self-care. When you can say "no" to things that don't align with who you are, you automatically make time and space for the things that do align. Saying "no" is not easy; it is an acquired skill for some. We all have been in a place in life—where we wanted to please people around us. Especially our children. We love them, but our yeses could hurt them in the long run if we're not careful about what we allow. Saying "yes" to everyone all the time is the best way to make our lives miserable. For this reason, we should be intentional with our "yes" and "no" responses.

You are responsible for creating your boundaries. Learning to say no is vital to keep you from dancing to the beat of someone else's drum. You aren't allowing others to control your time and actions. Instead, you're taking responsibility for yourself. You are also making others accountable for themselves with healthy boundaries and the ability to say no when something does not adhere to your limits.

Refusing something that does not complement who you are builds confidence and shows your respect for yourself. It can also strengthen your relationships as people begin to realize what it means to have a relationship with you. As a result, they become vigilant in respecting your decisions.

Saying no also brings you closer to living the life you want and being successful according to your definition of success. Research has shown that successful people have mastered the art of saying no, according to Ashley Stahl, a writer for *Forbes* magazine (2015, para. 11).

They understand the importance of staying focused, managing their time well, and being true to themselves. Anything that does not align with their goals is outside the realm of things they are willing to do.

That doesn't mean you have to be inconsiderate. It means you must consider the importance of saying yes and how your commitments will reflect your image and reveal your character; it ultimately lets people know if they can depend on you. So, if you are saying yes to things that you know you don't want to do, plan to get out of later, or you will regret later on, it could put a damper on your relationships. You will portray yourself as unreliable and someone who does not keep their word. You will also be causing yourself unnecessary stress. It is better to deal with the short-term discomfort that comes with saying no than with the long-term issues that come from saying yes to things you don't want to.

We understand that sometimes there can be pressure to answer someone who asks something of you, and to avoid making things awkward, you may want to answer in the way that best accommodates the other person. However, you don't have to feel bad for saying no.

You have the right to stand by your boundaries. Anyone who tries to make you feel bad for doing so probably does not have a good concept of boundaries or the ability to say no themselves. You can always take the time to think over your answer before giving one. If you don't know whether you want to say yes or no and need to evaluate the pros and cons, give yourself permission to weigh your options. Let the other person know you will think about it and get back to them. This communicates that you have heard their request and that you take whatever answer you give them seriously and will follow through on it. As we said, if you are not used to saying no, it will take some practice before you become comfortable doing it.

Mastering the Skill of Saying No

You do not have to be rude when saying no. You also don't have to explain yourself. "No" is a complete sentence, and it's okay if you treat it as such. However, here are some tips for saying "no" effectively and without being offensive:

Say It ...

Say It.

It seems obvious enough, but the first thing you need to know when it comes to saying no is just to say it. Speak clearly and confidently when saying it. Don't give supporting details or give in to the desire to make someone else feel good. Instead, be straightforward, honest, and integral.

Be Firm.

No matter what, do not go back on your "no." Doing so will make people believe they can always negotiate your boundaries. There will be a lack of respect for your word, so others will learn not to value it. This can lead to attempts to force or manipulate you into reconsidering where you stand. Let your "no" be "no" and your "yes" be "yes."

Sleep on It

An answer does not have to be immediate. With all the ways to communicate through technology now and its access to others, we may feel pressured to respond to people immediately, but this perceived notion is not valid. Take the necessary time you need to think about your answer. Let the other person know you will think about it and when you will get back to them, and be accountable for getting back to them at that time. With that being said, don't overthink your answer, either. If you have to think too hard about it, you probably shouldn't do it.

Give the Conversation Your Undivided Attention.

You don't want anyone to feel rejected or unimportant. So be sure to give your undivided attention to the conversation, even when just saying no. Sit or stand up straight and look the other person in the eyes. You want them to know you heard them and that you respect them.

Saying No to Your Partner

Saying no to your partner can be especially hard. You don't want to disappoint them, and you want to do whatever you can to keep them happy in the relationship. However, if your partner is unhappy, they must understand that happiness is an inside job. They must take the necessary steps to recognize their unhappiness and ultimately move toward happiness. They are responsible for their own emotions. You can ask probing questions to help them in their discovery journey.

Still, initially, if you can make someone happy, you can control every other aspect of their lives too, and this tinkers on the border of an unhealthy relationship.

Saying no establishes boundaries in a relationship and promotes health. If you and your partner cannot confidently say no to one another, it may be time to evaluate your boundaries and the health of your relationship. You say "no" to let people know who you are, and you should be able to show up 100% as that person in your relationship.

Saying no can protect mental and emotional well-being and create intimacy and a better support system within your relationship. It can also stimulate more positive than negative exchanges. You will have more time and energy to tend to yourself and, therefore, can better show up for your partner.

For example, you don't like going out with your partner and their friends because their friends aren't your kind of people.

The things they want to do and some of the things they say just don't sit well with you. Your partner was invited out with them and was told to bring you.

Your partner invites you, but you decline. You would rather spend your evening reading a good book and soaking in a nice bath. So, you politely refuse the offer by telling your partner "no." Instead of getting upset, your partner understands. They know the person you are, and you both have already established that their friends aren't your type of people, but you give your partner the freedom to be themselves and engage with their friends because they are their kind of people. You can spend your time doing things you love to do without the pressure of being someone you're not just to make the other person happy. This creates space for better mental and emotional well-being, as neither of you is stressed, angry, or resentful. So, it's a positive vibe when you are in each other's presence.

Chapter Summary ...

CHAPTER SUMMARY

If you are a people pleaser, make a point to stop being one as soon as possible. Practice saying no. It takes work, but it is a skill that can be acquired. You don't have to be rude or obnoxious when saying no. Neither does saying no make you rude or offensive. It means you value your time and energy and would rather spend it doing things that align with who you are and your goals.

Say no with confidence. Be firm, be fair, speak kindly and calmly, and give the other person your undivided attention. Be intentional about saying no just as much as you should be about saying yes. Remember that your word is your bond. If you don't stick to what you say, you run the risk of others not taking you seriously. Respect yourself if you want to see others respect you. You tell them who you are and not the other way around.

Don't let them control your life. Permit yourself to say no when you need to Say no it shows accountability, which is vital in relationships. You can start today to get some practice in.

Worksheet Activity …

Please take time to complete the worksheet below.

Saying No Worksheet

https://bit.ly/NoWorksheet

Chapter 8: Step 4—Taking Responsibility for Your Actions... and Words

So shall my word be that goeth forth out of my mouth: it shall not return unto me void, but it shall accomplish that which I please, and it shall prosper in the thing whereto I sent it. **Isaiah** 55:11, **KJV**,

I T CAN BE EASY to play the blame game. At some point in our lives, it has been our favorite game to play. However, the blame game isn't just about pointing fingers at others. Instead, it is our way of escaping the responsibility of being accountable for our actions and words and for being responsible for ourselves.

Here's the thing: Healthy relationships are built with two accountable individuals coming together as "one" to do life together. Joining the "us" team and out of the individualist society. You both have to be responsible for yourselves to show up for your partners.

Corinthians 13:11, KJV,

When I was a child, I spoke as a child, I understood as a child, and I thought as a child: but when I became a man, I put away childish things.

Most people think they have grown up because they are older, in the 20, 30, or even Over 50yrs of age. However, past trauma can trigger the childish version to continue into adulthood if we don't know how to control it. As Terrence Real Explains in his new book "Us," two versions of you might show up in your relationship: Do you bring the Adaptive child Version of you to the relationship? A child's version of an adult that you put together as a child. Triggered by the "past" that comes to the present- and turns into me against you mode in the relationship, and you make childish decisions?

Do you bring the Wise Adult Version of yourself to the relationship, where you'll be more empathetic and present? Again, it's about "Us," not " you against me" mode; you make wiser decisions. You must put aside childish ways, don't get offended so easily. It's not an attack on you. All you can change is your reaction. You should choose the Wise Adult.

You can be an individualist with a righteous stance or honoring person with a relational standpoint. You can't be both! One will keep the house at peace and help you rest at night. While the other will have you bickering and arguing, building up resentment, and it will start to divide the house and spill onto your children. You know, the crazy thing is that our perceptions of what we heard or didn't hear may be the thing that triggered us.

The Feedback wheel can help you with this! The Feedback Wheel is a tool that enables individuals to take responsibility for their actions, thoughts, and emotions and ask for what they need.

It has four steps: 1) describe the facts, 2) share your perception, 3) express how you feel, and 4) state what you want to happen in the future.

The Feedback Wheel has four steps.

1. The first step requires sticking to the facts, being objective, and speaking from your perspective.

1. The second step is your subjective interpretation of the situation.

1. Step three is identifying how you felt about the situation. It's important to differentiate between feelings and beliefs.

1. The fourth step is asking for what you want, taking responsibility for moving beyond your hurt, and asking your partner what they can do to help you.

Here's some example:

Let's say that you are upset with your partner because they didn't show up on time for a dinner reservation you had made.

Here's how you can use the Feedback Wheel to communicate your feelings effectively:

- Step 1: Stick to the facts and speak from your perspective

"I made a reservation for us at 7 pm, but you didn't show up until 7:30 pm."

- Step 2: Share your subjective interpretation of the situation

" I felt frustrated because I had made plans and was looking forward to spending time with you."

- Step 3: Identify how you felt about the situation

" I felt disrespected because you didn't show up on time."

- Step 4: Ask for what you want and take responsibility for moving beyond your hurt.

" In the future, can you please let me know if you're running late? It would help me feel more respected and valued in our relationship."

Here's another example:

When your partner stays out all night without communicating with you or picking up the phone:

Step 1: Stick to the facts and speak from your perspective

"You didn't come home last night and didn't even call to let me know where you were. I also tried calling you multiple times, but you didn't answer."

Step 2: Share your subjective interpretation of the situation

" I felt worried, anxious, and mad because I don't know if you were safe or if something happened to you. I also feel like you're not prioritizing our relationship when you don't answer my calls and stay out."

Step 3: Identify how you felt about the situation"

I feel disrespected, unimportant, and hurt because it seems like you didn't consider my feelings or our relationship. I also feel like you're not being honest with me."

Step 4: Ask for what you want and take responsibility for moving beyond your hurt

"It would mean a lot to me if you could communicate with me when you're going to be out late, and if you could answer my calls or at least let me know that you're okay.

I respect you enough to do the same for you. We have to talk about how we can work together to build more trust and respect in our relationship. If we are to make this relationship work"

The Feedback Wheel is a powerful tool for effective communication and can help bring about greater harmony and understanding in your relationships. When used correctly, You can communicate our feelings and needs in a clear and compassionate way. This helps create a safe and respectful space for both parties to express themselves.

We can create a deeper connection and trust with others by taking responsibility for our feelings and asking for what we need.

We hope this is of good use to you! Check out Youtube for more info on the feedback wheel!

The Subtle Art of Accountability ...

The Subtle Art of Accountability

Sacrifice can't be a side thing in a romantic or any relationship. You both have a role to play. While what one does affects the other person, each party is responsible for holding up their end of the bargain. Walking away from a relationship can be easier than taking responsibility for your actions. However, doing so will make you only face the same challenges if you decide to move to another relationship.

People who struggle with being accountable may have commitment issues, do things that overstep their partner's boundaries, or even be self-absorbed. All of these things have the potential to ruin a relationship. So how can you know if you struggle to be accountable for yourself? Here are some ways accountability issues may appear in a relationship:

Ghosting.

As we mentioned, people who don't want to be accountable for their actions may be more prone to end a relationship without letting the other person know. They may stop responding to messages, phone calls, and emails and even block the person on social media. People who do this may be running from a mistake they made or a fear of being uncomfortable by being honest with the other person. Suppose you struggle with accountability and have found yourself doing this even once. In that case, you can counter this action by intentionally being honest with yourself and others.

For example, you can practice what you want to say to the other person by writing a speech and practicing it in the mirror. Then, you can partner with a friend who may allow you to practice on them. You can also seek advice on how to share the uncomfortable truth with someone.

Not Being "Official

Be you; just keep it real. When you meet someone, let that someone know what you are and aren't looking for and why. Express your fear of commitment and be honest about why. If someone tries to force something on you that you are not ready for, you have the right to end things but don't just ghost them.

You also don't need to string them along. Be honest about why you can't continue seeing them. Be accountable for your role in ending things.

Too Busy for Relationships.

Sometimes, relationships are indeed worth more effort than we're willing to put in. We would rather spend our time doing other things because, let's face it, we make time for what we want, and if we don't want a relationship, we won't make time for it. But, on the other hand, there may be other reasons why we don't want a relationship, and we blame it on not having enough time.

We must be honest with ourselves and others about why we don't want to be in a relationship. Using the excuse of not having enough time is not being accountable.

Please take time to complete the worksheet below.
Are You Ready For the Commitment Quiz
Access it by Scanning the Qr code or visiting the link below.
https://bit.ly/CommitmentReady

Cheating

Sometimes, we may feel unfulfilled in a relationship, want to end things, and need to figure out how. Of course, the easy way out would be to cheat. However, regardless of how easy this option is, it is traumatic and harmful to the other person.

If you are the cheater, evaluate why you feel the need to step out of your relationship and determine what a more healthy response would be. Either you can choose to talk through your issues with your partner, or you can choose to leave, but choosing the option to cheat is not being accountable for your actions or your role in a relationship.

The Ingredients of a Strong Relationship

Relationships are formed when two people operate on the same frequency. Glitches happen. And when they do, it takes effort from both people to ensure the relationship stays intact. Playing the victim card can be easier than being accountable when things go wrong. Unfortunately, doing this only makes things worse. Here is what it takes to make sure your relationship stays strong and healthy:

Guard Your Tongues and must the most important Ingredient.

Those who guard their mouths and their tongues keep themselves from calamity. Proverbs 21:23 NIV

This bible verse, combined with Proverbs 15:1-2 serves us daily and is the foundation that keeps our relationship strong daily. This is not easy; some days, it may be challenging.

But, the crazy thing about life is you choose your hard. We encourage you to read more of the Proverbs; it will serve you well.

Emotional Responsibility.

You have to "be intentional" about being responsible for your emotions. When we get into relationships, sometimes we automatically think that the other person has to be responsible for us.

This mindset creates an unhealthy dependence on one another and removes all the fun and essential things from the relationship. Making your partner responsible for your emotions means you will never care for yourself how you need to. Then you may engage in the things that make you happy outside of your relationship; you won't see the importance of you and your partner being whole individuals in a union becoming one. Making your partner responsible for your emotions makes everything off balance in a relationship. They can help you on your journey.

Please take time to reflect and take action by completing the worksheets.

- The Emotional Bank Account For Couples Action Plan

Scan the Qr code or visit the link below before moving to the book's next chapter.
https://bit.ly/emotionalbank

Kindness, Acceptance, Compassion, and Empathy

In a strong relationship, you look out for each other. You accept your partner's unique qualities and understand what makes them who they are. You also allow them to compliment you. You aren't blinded by jealousy and envy but are supportive of your partner. You like that they are strong in the areas where you are weak and vice versa. Your relationship is a true partnership, as it should be. You share everything. There is no I in the word team.

You also are understanding when your partner makes a mistake. You are reasonable and loving still. You help lift them up when they are down. You aren't all about yourself in the relationship. You're considerate of your partner. You are kind to them and care for them in ways only you can as their partner. You will be their best friend. You know your partner better than anyone, which can be used to your advantage when it comes to serving them in any way.

If you don't have this in your relationship, there won't be love and respect. You may also lose trust in one another to be careful with each other's hearts and consider each other's feelings. Without a sense of security in these areas, loneliness, arguments, and even distance may exist. This will also keep you from fully submitting to your partner.

When you are compassionate toward one another, kind, caring, accepting, and empathetic, you lower your risk of having these issues or strengthen your chances of quickly finding solutions to the problems if they arise.

Warmth, Affection, Connection, Laughter, and Fun

This is one of the most precious things we do in our relationship that keeps us close. Having fun is vital in every relationship. It keeps you looking on the brighter side and keeps the spark between you. You want to find things to do together that you enjoy or just do something where you can enjoy one another's company. It's okay to do things together that distract you from the seriousness of life, but you always want to make sure you find time to connect. If you are not connecting regularly, this can also bring distance between you in your relationship.

Have Date Nights... and Alone Time.

You must stay connected with each other. Don't be one of those couples who can be in each other's presence yet be so distant by phone and video game systems. Instead, remember to enjoy each other daily.

Go on dates, spend time in each other's presence, and be present with no phone. Take a week's vacation, and make the time to date your partner at least 1-4 times a month. However, alone time is just as important. If you want to bring 100% to the relationship. Otherwise, you will lose stamina and find yourself trying to give from a half-full cup.

So pour into yourself as much as you pour into your relationship. Then those date nights will become so much more significant and memorable.

Conflict = Growth Opportunity.

When you face conflicts in your relationship, and you will, you should look at them as opportunities to learn from your mistakes and grow. They shouldn't make you feel depleted; instead, they should challenge you to improve. And take the customer service approach to grow through the conflict. This only works if both of you are trying to learn and apply what you have learned. If one person always puts a foot forward to grow and do better and the other does not, you become better and outgrow your partner. And that's not good. If you two are not growing together as a unit, then it may be time to rethink some things regarding your relationship.

Reciprocity

Healthy and strong relationships have reciprocity. What one gives, the other is willing to give in return. This also means that what one is feeling or experiencing, the other is willing to feel and experience it with them. If one is joyful, the other is joyful as well. There is no jealousy or envy in a healthy and strong relationship. You both understand that when one of you wins, you both win, and when one of you loses, you both lose. You're a team. It isn't a competition between the two of you.

"If a house is divided against itself, that house will not be able to stand" (Mark 3:24, ESV).

Intimacy

This is a big one. We want to avoid being superficial or dull in our relationship. We do this by connecting on deeper levels. Intimacy is created through trust, communication, love, and acceptance, and strong relationships have it. Intimacy can be physical, mental, emotional, and spiritual. Having sex, holding hands, kissing, and hugging are all physical intimacy. Even coming home after a long day of work and rubbing each other's pain spots can be considered physical intimacy. And it is just as important as being intimate in different ways.

Mental and emotional intimacy comes through respect and appreciation of each other's thoughts and feelings. When you can accept that your partner thinks differently than you do, ironically, you can agree on more things.

When you get that they see things differently and feel things differently than you do, then you learn about each other more, and you connect even more profoundly. Intimacy comes in different forms, but you want to ensure you acknowledge each form's importance. You don't want to be more intimate in one area and neglect others—for example, if you are constantly having sex but never mentally stimulating each other.

Maybe you're always talking about your feelings but never following through on them with a bit of physical touch. "Intimacy is a must, "but like everything else, it needs balance.

Not Making Comparisons

This goes back to what we were saying about no jealousy. Your jobs are to love, accept, and encourage each other to be your best. You shouldn't compare yourselves to one another, and to take it a bit further, you shouldn't be comparing your relationship to others' relationships. Everyone is running a different race in life. This can be hard because all you see are other people's relationships on social media. It may look good.

But your relationship is unique to you. So, embrace, enjoy, and remember that no one has a perfect relationship. So, don't go scrolling social media and wishing you could be like another couple. We don't know what goes on behind closed doors. Plus, the grass is never really greener on the other side. As we learn in chapter 2: The movie Tyler Perry's Temptation: Confessions Of A Marriage Counselor.

Chapter Summary ...

Chapter Summary

Being accountable in your relationship is essential. When you are responsible for yourself and what you do and say, you are allowing the opportunity for your relationship to be healthy and strong. You also set a standard for how you want to be treated. If you are accountable for yourself and considerate toward your partner, you remind them that you expect the same treatment in return.

Strong relationships aren't necessarily made up of strong people, only people willing to take risks and learn from their mistakes. A relationship is not a one-man band.

It is more like a business partnership. You each have roles and should be contributing in equal amounts.

The key word here is equal.

If you want a strong relationship, you need compassion, empathy, love, acceptance, intimacy, fun, and much communication. Strong relationships aren't built overnight. They go through processes. Building a strong relationship takes a lot of trial and error and, therefore, lots of almost daily forgiveness.

Worksheet Activity ...

Be sure to check out the book's action guide below this section.

- The Relationship Repairs Checklist

- Daily Checklist For Strengthening Your Relationship

You can access these worksheets below by Scanning the Qr code or visiting the link below.

Start using it to repair your relationship this week!
https://bit.ly/DailyLovecheck

https://bit.ly/ChecklistRepairs

Chapter 9: Step 5 — To Forgive Is Divine

"Forgiveness is the needle that knows how to mend." – Jewel.

F ORGIVENESS IS NOT A new concept. You may have heard many people talk about the idea of forgiveness. However easy it is to talk about forgiveness, it isn't an easy thing to do. Trust us. We know that forgiveness is essential to any person's healing process. Without forgiveness, you continue living in your past self-sabotage and ruin many relationships—even those that have the potential to be great. Revenge sometimes feels sweet. You want to get back at those people who hurt you. You want them to feel the same pain as you, but that is only a temporary temptation getting the best of you. It's not a method to heal your relationships. It's a recipe for burning bridges, not building them.

Forgiveness is never so much for the other person as it is for yourself, and we'll tell you why.

The Art of Forgiveness

Is so Hard, but it's cleansing your mind, soul, and spirit from the thoughts and pain of what someone else did to you, ultimately, things you cannot control. You can never control the actions of others. What you can control is how you respond to it. Forgiveness would be an adequate and loving response to any hurt inflicted upon you. You don't have to be a saint to practice forgiveness, nor should you be an over-thinker.

"Holding on to anger is like grasping a hot coal with the intent of throwing it at someone else; you are the one getting burned." — Rhonda Byrne.

The Importance of Forgiving People

When you hold anger and resentment toward someone, they have power over you. When you are fearful of someone, they hold power over you. Forgiveness sets you free from the unconscious control of others and allows you to live life on your own terms. It will enable you to continue your life journey authentically.

You also free people when you forgive them. You hold people's souls and spirits captive when you harbor unforgiveness toward them.

Though that may not bother you if revenge is your goal, keeping them captive does more harm to you than it does to them. It goes back to allowing them to control you. You are now walking around with pieces of them in you—the person you despise and probably want to be nothing like—and you may act the same way they did toward you. You may inflict some of the same pains on others or cause some of the same cycles.

Unforgiveness can chip away at your physical well-being just as much as your mental, emotional, and spiritual well-being.

Harboring hate, anger, and other negative feelings have been linked with high blood pressure, cancer, and other health conditions. Forgiving others is a part of self-care.

Forgiveness in romantic relationships is also crucial if you want a lasting, intimate relationship. Unforgiveness causes blockages. It causes people to put up walls; as discussed earlier, walls are not the same as fences. You can't get anything through a wall; you must break it down to see what's on the other side. Do you want your partner to exhaust themselves to get to your heart? If so, call the relationship quits and move on. What's the point of being together if you don't even want to try to let them in?

Forgiveness creates space for love to flow freely. It produces peace and simplicity in your relationship and within your being. When you forgive your partner, you open communication avenues and allow for trust to be rebuilt in those areas. These are relevant components of any relationship, let alone a romantic relationship.

What You Need to Know About Forgiving

Forgiveness takes time, effort, and some elbow grease. You have to be a certain kind of dedicated to accomplishing forgiveness. And you have to be patient because it is a process. Be patient with yourself, and be patient with the other person. It doesn't happen overnight; even when you think you have forgiven, more work still needs to be done.

You may find this out if you are triggered down the road.

Acknowledge where you are in your process at all times and communicate that with your partner.

Be open, honest, and willing to receive their input if necessary. Be vulnerable. Be authentic, and don't compare your journey to anyone else's because you'll only end up disappointing yourself. So, what about forgiveness makes it so simple yet so complex at the same time?

Gratitude

You probably hear it so much that it sounds cliché, but practicing gratitude makes forgiveness more attainable. When looking at the brighter side of things, you have less time and energy to put into gazing at the negatives.

"Gratitude is the great multiplier." — Rhonda Byrne.

Gratitude makes your heart smile. When you count your blessings, you remember the beauty of life. We all come from somewhere. Remembering where you came from usually helps with gratitude as you look at your life and see your progress over the years, even if it won't seem like it on the surface.

Please take time to connect some pieces by completing the worksheet below.

Partner Appreciation Worksheet below

Scan the Qr code or visit the link below to access

https://bit.ly/Pappriciate

Develop Compassion

When someone hurts you, it is hardly ever because of you. It's what they're battling on the inside of themselves. There are two main emotions that every action usually stems from. They are love and fear (Nelson, 2019, para. 8). When someone acts out of fear, they do hurtful things. They cause damage, and they create unhealthy cycles. They can be a menace to society, honestly. However, you can always look deeper than the action and get underneath the surface to discover the real problem. If you decide to keep your relationship intact, imagine how loving that person through their mistakes would build trust, deepen intimacy, and even be the encouragement the person needs to do better next time.

Perspective

Sometimes, our perspectives are the things causing us pain. If we look at things from a victim mindset, we become victims. Don't get us wrong now; there is nothing wrong with feeling like you have been wronged, especially if you have been! But there comes the point when you have to want to take responsibility for your healing and stop pointing fingers. Could you have played a role in the happenings? If so, what do you need to change or do better at? Again, what can you learn from this? Have a growth mindset, always. Challenges come to make you stronger, not to take you out. Don't give up on yourself.

Forgive Yourself First

Many times, the first person we need to forgive is ourselves. You may beat yourself up for allowing certain things to happen to you. You may feel inadequate, insignificant, foolish, and other harmful things. Forgive yourself. You could not have known better beforehand, even though now you do. Be gracious with yourself. Give yourself the benefit of the doubt and trust yourself again. Free yourself from negative thinking patterns due to someone else's insignificant actions. You are accountable for yourself and no one else.

How to Be More Forgiving …

HOW TO BE MORE **Forgiving**

If we're being honest, you will have to do forgiveness every day of your life. Some things will be easier to forgive than others. You may internalize some things without realizing it until you consciously begin healing yourself.

Though it is easy to break trust and more challenging to build, staying open to the possibility of your partner growing and becoming better daily is needed for the relationship to be long-lasting. While it may not be easy to forget, we should always strive to forgive. Forgiveness allows for communication to remain truthful and authentic.

It is understandable to have a little fear, but strong relationships are secure. If you are insecure in your relationship, it may be time to look at your communication to see if it could use some work.

Being forgiving is a mindset, a heart posture, and a soul purification. There's a saying: The weak never forgive, and the strong don't forget. You can't expect to be happy if you're sad from the inside. You must learn to let go of a few things to live freely. Forgiveness doesn't come naturally. It's more of a practiced art that requires attention to the following points:

Don't Internalize Blame.

While you want to refrain from pointing fingers at others so you can heal properly, you also don't want to blame yourself unnecessarily. This can also be a hindrance to your healing. It keeps you from forgiving yourself and possibly allowing the same hurtful behavior again. It will limit your ability to set boundaries and care for yourself mentally and emotionally.

Be Honest

It's easier to forgive something if you don't allow the feelings toward it to build up. Be honest about how something makes you feel when the feelings arise in the right environment. This allows you and your partner to talk through the emotions and develop solutions to prevent future issues. And not cover up the problem.

As we learn in Chapter 1 from Ralph and Emma, that can be a recipe for *Disasters*. It also creates an opportunity for you and your partner to connect. It increases your intimacy levels when you both can be vulnerable and understanding.

Allow Yourself to Heal

Healing is a process. It happens with time. It isn't something that comes by you trying to sweep the issues under the rug. It comes by facing the problems and dealing with them firsthand. Accept and embrace how you feel. Allow yourself to feel everything fully and then take steps to render those feelings. Cry if you must get by yourself and Cry; let it out. The more you let it out, the more pain you release. Talk to someone if you need to, maybe a therapist who can help you work through your trauma. This can be instant healing for some and may work for you.

Don't try to rush your process. Be honest with your partner about where you are and how they can accompany you on your journey to healing because they cannot heal you. That is your responsibility. They can only be your support while you put in the necessary work.

If you and your partner are working toward mending your relationship after an unforgiving situation, don't feel compelled to forgive and trust them again immediately. Take your time, be patient, and enjoy the process. It isn't just about the destination but also how you get there. Don't let the journey make you forget the brighter side of things. Remember to practice gratitude.

Make Rebuilding a Mutual Effort

Rebuilding trust and allowing forgiveness to make its way into your relationship takes effort on both ends. Make necessary apologies, have hard conversations, be understanding and compassionate, and be willing to take risks to achieve forgiveness.

It can be scary to open your heart again to someone who hurt you, and that's where the boundaries come into play. Trusting yourself with your partner's heart can also be difficult once you have hurt them, as feelings of inadequacy can swoop in. Depending on which side of the spectrum you are on.

Express what you're experiencing to your partner so you can work together to help each other through it. And the great thing about it is that you two can set the pace. Once you get on the same page, you can accomplish everything. We know you can!

Keep Moving Forward

The thoughts of those heartbreaking moments may continue returning. Until they no longer negatively affect you, you must be intentional about not responding negatively to those thoughts. Stay busy; distract yourself by doing something you enjoy or thinking about something that makes you happy. Also, refrain from bringing the issue back up in future arguments when you're trying to heal and move forward. You have to allow your partner the opportunity to redeem themselves if you are giving your relationship another try. Throwing their failures up in their face every time you're mad will discourage them from doing that.

Don't punish them. If you want to move forward and a big one, don't punish yourself. Let go of pride. It will kill you! It is hard to let go of pride, but getting a step closer to forgiving is necessary. Pride is the biggest thing that keeps us from moving forward. We stay stagnant because we don't want to admit it hurts. We have needs and struggles and don't want to be where we are.

Take Your Time

They say time heals all wounds. We don't know about all of them, but we can agree on most, anyway. There are some things that time does not heal the pain of, and in those cases, it takes a lot of grace to accept your struggle and embrace your process because you may encounter painful memories for a lifetime. However, just because the wound hasn't gone away doesn't mean it can't fade to a faint line. You don't have to live your whole life walking around with a limp because you have scars, but you can embrace the fact that the scars aren't going anywhere, and you can still love yourself with those scars. This means finding healthy ways to cope until it no longer affects you negatively, until you become grateful for the experience, and use the pain to push you forward.

Chapter Summary ...

Chapter Summary

When things happen that negatively affect your emotional health, when you are betrayed and hurt, or when you find it hard to forgive, remember that you have an opportunity ahead of you to start fresh. Even though it may not be with them, you don't have to continue the relationship if you don't want to, but if you decide to move forward with the person that caused you pain, you are making a conscious decision to put in the effort every day to forgive them.

Forgiveness is a process and does not happen overnight or by saying "I forgive you" out loud. Forgiveness becomes a way of life as you become intentional about your healing, serious about your boundaries, and more caring toward yourself. You also choose to be compassionate, kind, caring, and understanding with the person who hurt you. You decide to move past the hurt, regardless of what it takes.

When thoughts arise that remind you of what happened, you replace them with positive thoughts. You make the conscious decision not to act on the hurtful feelings the thoughts bring.

When you are struggling to see the brighter side of things, you intentionally shift your mind, analyzing the situation from a neutral standpoint and gaining an understanding of what drove the action to hurt you. You decide to look past your fears and be authentically you. You make the conscious decision to be open, honest, and communicative with the person who hurt you, let it out, but you don't throw the wrongdoing back in their face. Instead, you give them a chance to redeem themselves. You become reasonable and fair in your actions. And although you forgive, you don't dare to force yourself to forget. Instead, you harness the power to make something good from the negative.

Ultimately you take your power back when you forgive, which is why it is so important. Then, you wake up each day with a fresh attitude and optimism toward the future. What happened yesterday is a part of your story, but it doesn't have to be the determining factor in who you are. You can walk in today and close the door to yesterday behind you; it's up to you. We know you can do it!

Worksheet Activities ...

Take some time to complete the book's action guide below this section.

Moving on from the past hurts

VULNERABILITY EXERCISE

You can access the worksheet below by Scanning the Qr code or visiting the link below.

https://bit.ly/VulnerableEXERCISE

https://bit.ly/PastHurtss

Chapter 10: Step 6—Close the Door Behind You

"Don't let failure or disappointment cut you off from God or make you think that the future is hopeless. When God closes one door, He often opens another door - if we seek it." ~ Billy Graham

T HE CHALLENGES WE FACE are meant to strengthen us, help us grow, and encourage us to become more of the people we were created to be. It can be hard to remember this in the face of those challenges. If we experience traumatic events as children without the proper support, we can suffer from PTSD, and our adult relationships can be severely affected. Sometimes things happen to us that traumatize us so badly that we live wounded, or we don't even realize we have been affected so much by it. Our wounds become our reality. We have to close the door to that and move on. And not be held captive by our old selves but embrace the new.

We all have a past. Some memories are sweet, and some are too dark to want to remember. Regardless, the past will always stick with us to some degree and affect our decision-making abilities and outlook toward life. It doesn't mean that sewing the wounds of the past is impossible, though.

Healing your wounds starts with recognizing that you are wounded and not living fully.

Here are some of the signs of unhealed wounds.

Anxiety

Being anxious or extremely nervous about what could go wrong means you are afraid of something. Fear can result from past traumas that were not dealt with properly. Signs of anxiety include being fidgety, having restless thoughts, an inability to sleep well, and even having anxiety attacks in relatively normal or stressful situations. People who deal with anxiety may also engage in risky behaviors such as drinking and smoking to ease the thoughts in their minds and calm them down.

Some people don't realize it, but it isn't necessarily the inhalation of smoke that calms them, but more so the breathing. When you are feeling anxious, try deep breathing to calm yourself so that you can think clearly and possibly rest your thoughts on something more positive.

Shame

Traumatic events can make you feel inadequate. You can wonder why a certain thing happened to you. You may want to hide behind your ego and a fake smile. If you are a prideful person, look underneath your pride and see if you discover a shameful being who is scared that people will see them. Ask yourself why you're afraid of people seeing who you are. Did something happen to you to make you not like that person?

Depression

Unhealed wounds can make looking at the brighter side of things hard. There may be an underlying issue if you always feel gloomy and down. There are different ways to deal with depression. You can care for yourself more by intentionally eating healthy and staying active. You can talk to a therapist. There are also medicines out there that are designed to treat depression.

Avoidance

Sometimes, when a person has experienced trauma and is afraid of experiencing it again—or anything remotely close to it—they will avoid people and situations that remind them of it.

Addiction

As mentioned before, when we experience trauma, our first thought is to escape it. We don't want to feel the pain of it anymore. We don't even want to remember it. So, indulging in anything that distracts us and provides an escape, such as drugs, alcohol abuse, overeating, or binge-watching television. But, unfortunately, if indulging in any of these behaviors, you may have unhealed wounds.

Disassociation

This borders along the lines of avoidance. When a person dissociates themselves, they isolate themselves from others. They become less relatable, less understanding, less forgiving, and unwilling to create meaningful relationships. As a result, they tend to feel alone in life as well. If it is hard for you to have meaningful conversations, connect with others, or maintain meaningful relationships because you run at the sign of the slightest problem, you could have unhealed wounds.

Self-Harm

People who harm themselves have not quite grasped how to handle the pain they are experiencing, and most times, they just want to make it stop. Some people have admitted to self-harm. Do it because they say it feels good.

It isn't that it feels good; it's that it distracts them from their traumatic experience and gives them an outlet to release the pain they are already feeling. These people may be harboring anger and resentment. It is a sign that past wounds still need healing.

Inability to Focus

Trauma can take over your mind. If you tend to forget things easily, your mind wanders a lot, and you can't stay focused or pay attention, you could still be suffering from that traumatic event.

Lack of a Will to Live

Along with depression and anxiety, some people report feeling dead inside, like they have no purpose or that their life is meaningless. They dread living and can't find a reason why they still wake up every day. They may feel hopeless or like nothing matters anymore, leading them to make irrational decisions and not care anymore. If you have experienced similar feelings, you may now know why.

Healing Old Wounds

Healing is a process. It is a matter of will and grace. Are you willing? And will you give yourself the grace to do it? There is hope if you're stuck with past problems and want to break free.

What old wounds do you need to heal from?

Use these tips to jumpstart your healing process:

Start Small

Trying to do everything at once can be a recipe for disaster. You don't need grand gestures or to try to get there fast. Start small. Slow and steady wins the race. Ever heard that? It is true, so pace yourself. Don't think you must start your process today and wake up tomorrow healed. It doesn't work that way, and expecting that could lead you to overwhelm yourself and lose the drive to keep going. Take your time.

Be Consistent

Consistency is key. Consistency is key. You may not see results for a while. You could encounter challenges that make it seem like you are experiencing setback after setback. Remember, every setback is a setup for a comeback. There's a brighter tomorrow on the other side of a gloomy day. And look forward to it. Every day will take a lot of work, and it won't be all sunshine and rainbows. Some days there will be rain and thunderstorms. This is what the healing process looks like. Keep going. Things will start looking up permanently soon.

Set Realistic Goals

Big goals are achieved through a series of smaller goals. Set small, achievable goals to reach your goal of being healed of a wound or traumatic event. Don't stay in the cycle of going from goal to goal. Instead, celebrate small wins to give yourself the boost you need to keep going. For us or the wifey taking trips is our way of Celebrating small wins. If you're all business and no fun, you risk forgetting that the whole point is to live your most fun, fulfilling life.

Plus, you'll be healing from something for the rest of your life. Don't let that make your life dull. Be joyous in the process.

Learn From Experiences ...

Learn From Experiences

Every experience comes with a lesson. Dig deep to find what the lesson is and embrace it. Be ready to apply what you learn as well. What good is knowing something if you won't put it to use?

" Wisdom is the principal thing; Therefore, get wisdom. And in all your getting, get understanding. Exalt her, and she will promote you; She will bring you honor when you embrace her. She will place on your head an ornament of grace; A crown of glory she will deliver to you." NKJV Proverbs 4:7-9

When bad things happen, it is hardly ever just because bad things happen. There is a lesson buried deep somewhere, waiting to be discovered. If someone hurts you, what is the experience trying to bring out of you? Reveal to you? Instead of asking why something happened to you and taking on the victim role, become the captain of your ship by taking control of your thoughts and asking yourself, "What can this experience teach me?" Use the opportunity to grow and become a better you versus allowing it to make you bitter, mean, hateful, and ugly. That's not doing anything but giving up on yourself; you should never do that. Fight to the finish!

Take some time to complete the book's action guide below this section in the book.

Lessons Learned Worksheet
Scan the Qr code or visit the link below for access

https://bit.ly/lessonslearnedd

Take Care of Yourself ...

TAKE **C**ARE OF **Y**OURSELF.

Remember to tend to your needs during this process. Healing requires daily self-care. In what ways can you take care of yourself? Can you eat more fruits and veggies? Could you benefit from more exercise? Can you turn off your phone at a specific time every day to get some quiet time? Could you be intentional about spending time with those that you love?

One of the things my wife and I do in the morning in our self-care routine has become spiritual growth and personal healing for us. And you need both. Our day doesn't go right if we don't first listen to "grace for purpose" and "Let's Become Successful, "both on youtube. It helps us start the day off by being intentional. Take care of the mind and heart to keep you open for the spiritual! The closer you get to God, the healthier you become.

What about setting boundaries for others and yourself? Do whatever you can to tend to your daily needs and care for yourself. This makes the process feel smoother on days when it seems to all be going to hell. Don't neglect yourself. Love yourself, and surround yourself with a community of good people.

Accept What Was and What Is.

What happened to you happened. All you can do now is accept it and close that chapter of your book of life. You cannot change it, and it would not be wise to run from it. It does nothing but makes the problems worse. Acceptance is the first step to healing; you must complete all the steps in this process. I want you to know you have to go through them all.

Accept Help

It can be hard to admit we need help, let alone ask for it. For trauma survivors, sometimes asking for help feels like burdening someone, or they could be too ashamed to let people see where they're struggling. The thing is, we are meant to help each other. Why do you think there are so many people on this earth? Who can you trust to help you? Would you benefit from getting professional help? Of course, being in a funk is part of the process as well, but if you find yourself stuck there, seek the help you need to get out of there.

It doesn't make you any less strong because you need a helping hand. We all do every once in a while. It's what makes us human. Your partner can be the first one to help.

Healing your wounds starts with recognizing that you are wounded and not living fully.

Take some time to complete the book's action guide below this section.

List Of Little Things For Couples Worksheet
Scan the Qr code or visit the link below in the book to access

https://bit.ly/littlethingss

Signs of Recovery

There is a way to measure your recovery against your wounds. Look back on where you came from to where you are, and smile if you notice any changes. Be grateful you aren't where you were; even though you aren't where you want to be, you have come a long way. Celebrate that!

Here are some ways to know if you are recovering:

You're Getting Better with Your Feelings.

You acknowledge your feelings when they arise, and immediately you name them. You keep control of your emotions by expressing them appropriately and healthily instead of bottling them up. You talk about them instead of ignoring them and pretending they aren't there, and you talk about them.

You're Over the Blame Game

You understand that stuff happens and that, ultimately, you have a responsibility to yourself as much as others have a responsibility to themselves. You don't try to control or blame others unnecessarily, and you don't take on all the blame. You use challenges as an opportunity for growth and accountability versus making yourself a victim or becoming the source of other people's pain.

You Trust More

Trust is hard to rebuild after it has been broken. Sometimes traumatic experiences can make you even lose trust in yourself. However, when you are recovering well, you will notice that trust comes more frequently, and you are more open to the possibility of things going right than wrong.

You trust others to do well until they give you a reason not to, and even then, you work toward trusting again because you understand that they're human and will make mistakes. And you give yourself that same grace.

You Give Yourself Permission to Have a Voice.

If you find yourself being more assertive, speaking up for yourself, or speaking up for what you believe in, it may be because you are on the road to recovery. So keep up the good work; we know you got this!

You Handle Rejection Well

Rejection can hurt even the healthiest, most emotionally secure of us. How you handle that hurt speaks volumes, though. If you find yourself responding less negatively to rejection, that is a good sign.

You Aren't Easily Angered

Many traumatized people are offended and much more defensive than usual. On the other hand, someone recovering may harbor more peace and illuminate more peace. They won't be easily angered by things.

You Respect Boundaries

When you understand how important boundaries are, you begin to respect other people's boundaries. You know they are a means of self-care and protection, and you make yourself accountable to others if they communicate those boundaries to you. You don't feel entitled or try to force people to step outside of their boundaries for you. You are not threatened by other people's boundaries; you support them. As a result, you're more prone to treating people how you want to be treated and being considerate when recovering well.

You're More Confident

You can look at yourself in the mirror and be proud of yourself. You are happy with the person you are and are becoming. You look forward to that person with optimism. You believe in yourself. Your traumatic experience no longer has the power to make you feel like you're less than enough or to make you feel ashamed. You are free to love yourself when you are recovering well.

You Get Stuff Done

One of the signs that you are still wounded is procrastination—oddly enough. When you are on the road to recovery, you tend to manage your time better. You set goals and work toward them diligently. You may have an objective for each day, and you aim to complete that objective by the time your head hits the pillow that night. You also understand that as long as you give each day your best, it is okay if you do not accomplish everything. You do your best, and you acknowledge that. Celebrate what you achieve each day, and try again tomorrow. You're dedicated and persistent.

Chapter Summary ...

Chapter Summary

Yesterday is indeed gone, and today is a new day. That does not mean that yesterday's troubles automatically disappear with the day, like fading credits at the movie's end. To live in today and be hopeful for tomorrow is not easy as 1,2,3, though there are steps you can take toward your healing. First, learn what it looks like when you have un-healed wounds, then evaluate your past traumas and determine what you need healing from.

Accept that there is a process to healing and be determined to put in the necessary work. Soon you will find yourself on the road to recovery.

Healing is important when you and your partner actively seek ways to mend your relationship and possibly build something new together.

Worksheet Activities ...

Complete the book's action guide below this section.

Self-Awareness Writing Exercise

Access Your Readiness For Emotional Intimacy

Scan the Qr code or visit the link below before moving to the book's last chapter.

https://bit.ly/AWARENESSWRITING

https://bit.ly/READINESS4INTIMACY

Chapter 11: Step 7—Igniting Intimacy

"The opposite of Loneliness is not Togetherness, It's Intimacy" — **Richard Bach**

B ETRAYAL HURTS, ESPECIALLY WHEN it is by someone you love dearly. When you and your partner are going through a rough time, and your relationship has hit a sour patch, you may be desperate for things to be sweet again. Negative emotions can be at their peak, but rest assured that this does not have to be the end if you don't want it to be. You get to decide where you want to go next.

The Three Phases of Recovery

There are three recovery phases. You will go through each one while mending what has been broken in your relationship. They are the crisis phase, insight phase, and vision phase.

Once you have gone through the phases, you can begin enjoying what you and your partner are building together and see that your hope for better (and ultimately all the hard work you put in) was not in vain.

Crisis Phase

This is the rockiest phase of them all. Your emotions may be up and down, and you may not quite understand them. You and your partner may find yourselves pulling closer in the bedroom despite feelings of fear and pain. This is because the betrayal hurts but also makes you fear that what you want and who you want are in jeopardy. You may be longing for each other but unable to let go of the offense or betrayal (Nelson, 2019, para. 4). This is normal. It shows that love is there but that there is also fear. You have to work through the fear to get to the next stage. But take your time.

Don't feel the need to rush it, or you might be back in the crisis stage. Be honest about where you are, how you feel, and what you want as much as possible.

Insight Phase

In this phase, you may be motivated to ask probing questions to ease your curiosity. You want to understand the why behind the action instead of being stuck on it. You want to know what went wrong and how you can work together to fix it. You'll still experience hurt in this phase, but it is easing each day with the more understanding you gain. So take it one day at a time and continue steadily toward your future together, should you decide to have one.

Vision Phase:

This is where you decide if you and your partner will continue. You will create a vision for how you want your future to look. This is when you establish new boundaries and set expectations.

It is when you are clear about what you need and want from your partner and what you can give. The vision stage starts your process of forgiveness and rebuilding trust because if you decide to stay together, you will need both of those to make your new relationship work. This is your chance at a new beginning, and you want to avoid bringing any of the filth of the old relationship into the new one you are creating together. Make the conscious decision to do the necessary work to embark on a journey beyond this phase.

The Connection Between Intimacy and Communication

Communication and intimacy are needed in a relationship's foundation to withstand the challenges of time. What if we told you that intimacy is necessary for you and your partner to communicate effectively, just as much as communication is needed to connect on a deeper level.

"Communication in love relationships is a result of connection" (How to fix a relationship, 2019, para. 19). Basically, to achieve effective communication in your relationship, there has to be understanding and a desire to connect on a deeper level. Communicating for any other reason and through any other lens takes away from the significance while negatively affecting your intimacy.

Still, without communication, it is impossible to have intimacy.

It takes communication between you and your partner to convey what you need and want from them. It takes communication to share what your love language is, and it takes communication to love your partner.

Whether we realize it or not, we constantly communicate verbally or nonverbally. Your partner communicates with you through body language and what they don't say just as much as they communicate with you in words. Sometimes it's hard to convey a message in words, but easy to share the same message with physical touch, listening intently, or even just eye contact if you want to show your partner that you are interested in them.

When it comes to communicating with words to create intimacy, it takes a lot more than the mundane, everyday conversations you have about simple things. Instead, you want to have deeper, heart-felt, soul-quenching conversations intentionally.

Think of some interesting conversation starters. Then pick your partner's brain. Ask about how they feel about a specific subject. Ask questions that require more than a yes or no answer. Whatever conversation path you choose to take, let the conversation flow smoothly. Be intentional but don't force results. Be authentic and listen intently when your partner speaks. Look them in the eyes. Hold hands while you talk. Use the time to watch for their nonverbal cues so that you can gain an understanding of their communication style. These are all ways to make a conversation more intimate.

Please take time to complete the worksheet below.

Revving Up The Romance In Your Relationship workbook

Sex And Intimacy Worksheet

Scan the Qr code or visit the link below before moving to the book's next chapter.

https://bit.ly/sexNintimacy

https://bit.ly/RevvingUpRomance

Rekindling the Intimacy ...

Rekindling the Intimacy

When you have been together for a while, as we have, things can begin to get dull without the proper daily TLC after you have left that honeymoon phase of your relationship. If you aren't intentional, your physical and emotional intimacy can take a hit, placing the relationship on thin ice for many couples. One or both of you may feel less connected, unsatisfied, unhappy, and craving more. You may miss that spark at the beginning, dimmed by all the everyday tasks of your simple but hectic life together. However, there is hope for you and a lifeline for your relationship. You don't have to go somewhere new whenever your life needs something fresh and you want to connect with someone. You can achieve that right where you are. Here's how:

Be Attentive.

Your partner has needs in the relationship just like you do. You can create a space where they feel their needs are being heard by paying attention to them—their nonverbal cues and listening intently when they speak. The more you listen, the better you can serve them. When you fill your partner in the way they need you to, it opens the door for connectivity to flow right in.

Not only will they feel more loved, considered, and understood, but they will also have the desire to reciprocate what you are giving.

Be Transparent

When you are transparent, you allow the other person to see all of you, the ugly and the beautiful. This can be scary, especially if your intimacy has been affected by broken trust. But it is needed to rebuild what has been torn down. Without vulnerability and willingness to let down your guard, you may never experience the connection you desire because you'll never get the chance to truly get close to one another.

You will have allowed fear to be the wall between you, ultimately keeping you from living two separate lives under the same roof. There is always the risk of being hurt when you allow yourself to be in love.

If you're already taking the risk of being in a loving relationship, you should go all in. Make it worth your time, and you may see your love withstand the trials of time.

Take the initiative

Sometimes, being the first to make a move is daunting, especially if you have yet to be as intimate as you'd like. You are still determining what it is that your partner will like. Next, you need to figure out what to say that they will be receptive to. If you need help figuring out where to start, ask. Sometimes it's just that simple. Be accountable and ask what they want to see from you and how you can make them feel more connected to you. This shows them that you care and is a step in a positive direction.

Be Realistic

Sometimes, our desire to have a fairy tale romance stands in the way of fully experiencing what is right in front of us, and what is right in front of us can be what we need if we let it be. Don't have too high of expectations that you miss out on something great for something that doesn't exist.

Be Supportive

We guarantee you that one of the main things your partner desires from you is acceptance. Accept who your partner is and who they are not. Encourage them to be themselves. Show them that they are not alone and you are in their corner. It makes connecting so much easier when a person feels like who they are is enough and they don't have to make a bunch of drastic changes to be accepted. Be their safe space.

Reflect and Assess Your Emotions

Having emotions is a part of life. It's part of being human. Even people who show their feelings less than average have them; they cannot express them properly. There is power in owning your emotions, though. First, think deeply about your feelings and determine why you feel them.

Next, decide if what you are feeling is worth it or not. Then, choose the best way to release those emotions— let them go or share them intently with your partner.

Sharing your emotions with one another doesn't always have to be negative. You can find creative ways to communicate with each other. For example, you can make sharing fun by turning it into a game. You can also use nonverbal cues to express how you're feeling.

For example, if you're feeling appreciative, you might hug your partner, kiss them, wink at them, or even high-five them. This not only allows you to be more emotionally connected but physically connected as well.

Get Uncomfortable

When things have dulled, take a moment to assess whether you and your partner have tried anything new recently. It's easy to get caught up in the normal. Routine is okay, but sometimes it is better to mix things up a little bit. Free yourself from the box you're so used to living in and make it a point to go outside what you're usually comfortable with. Your relationship could benefit from this.

Practice the 10-Minute Ritual ...

PRACTICE THE **10**-**M**INUTE **R**ITUAL

This is where you and your partner take 10 minutes out of your busy day or week to listen to each other. You can talk about anything you want during your 10 minutes. Speak your mind. During this time, the other person just listens with undivided attention. Listen intently, be engaged in what they are saying, and have eye contact. Avoid making nonchalant facial expressions while they are talking, even if you don't like what they are saying. Only speak when you want the speaker to explain more of what they just said.

You could talk or use the time to think about what to say without saying anything. You could do it for the whole 10 minutes if you choose to. Take time every day or week to connect with your partner the kids can benefit from this as well. This is meant to help you and your partner get better at listening to each other and getting to know each other better. Now, this exercise may be harder for men, but no worries, with practice, you get better. Plus, you'll be a step closer to healthier communication. I promise you this will do wonders for your family.

You can learn more about the process below by Scanning the Qr code
or visiting the link below in the book.

To 10-Minute Ritual 4-Step Process

https://bit.ly/4StepProcessritual

Learn How I Desire To Be Loved.

This will serve you well. How we give and receive love is connected with something called love language. Love language is unique to every individual. When you know your partner's love language, you can more readily love them how they need to be loved and be more understanding of how they show you that they love you and vice versa.

Gary Chapman has five love languages: acts of service, receiving gifts, words of affirmation, quality time, and physical touch. Here are some ways to show love in each language:

Acts of Service

Suppose this is your partner's love language. In that case, it might benefit you to do something like helping them with a project they are invested in but is stressing them out, taking on some of their daily chores when you notice they're exhausted, or offering them a massage to help them relax.

Receiving Gifts

The person with this love language just wants to know you are thinking of them. Even the smallest, inexpensive gift has meaning to them.

You could even pay some bills. Get together with your children and make them a thank you card. Buy them that slow cooker they've been raving about. Get them tickets to their favorite concert. The more thoughtful the gift, the better.

Words of Affirmation

This person wants to feel accepted and wants the same for others. Therefore, they are prone to feeling more loved when they are encouraged, praised, and reminded that they are an amazing person.

Quality Time

Spending downtime with this person shows them that you love them. They want to be in your presence, enjoying life together, doing fun things, or even doing nothing at all. It's about being with you and getting to know each other more through spending time together. Include them in your plans for a night out or run a bubble bath that you two will enjoy together. Watch your favorite movie or cook your favorite dish together.

Physical Touch

This type of person gives and receives love through physical affection. They receive love the best by holding hands, kissing, body rubs, or even just stroking their hair. This is also the way they give love.

Chapter Summary ...

Chapter Summary

Communication and intimacy go hand in hand. You can only have one with the other. For a woman, intimacy starts way before you get intimate. If you can just love your partner daily the way "they" want to be loved. You'll be amazed at the progress over time. Here's the thing, you don't need good communication skills as much as a connection to communicate well. However, you need to communicate to have a connection with your partner.

Communication is a constant daily thing. It happens verbally as well as nonverbally. Therefore, you can learn your partner's communication style and have a better chance of connecting with them on another level. It really is that simple.

Intimacy in your relationship keeps it alive. You recreate that spark you had in the beginning every time you choose to be intimate with your partner. Intimacy comes in different forms: emotional, physical, and mental. All of them are important. Abandoning one for the other leaves space for your partner to be unfulfilled. Which is not good.

You can practice being intimate by consciously making time for each other each day to talk about things that stimulate you—something outside of the typical daily tasks. The more you can do this on a daily the better.

You can be intentional about being physically close to each other by holding hands, hugging, touching, or giving massages. Sex is also important. Suppose the fire of intimacy was put out because of a betrayal of trust. In that case, it isn't and doesn't have to be the end of your relationship. With hard work and daily dedication, you can enjoy one another again.

Worksheet Activities ...

PLEASE TAKE TIME TO **reflect and take action by completing the worksheets.**

Love Languages For Couples Worksheet

Showing The Language of Love:

Life balance Action plan

Scan the Qr code or visit the link below before moving to the book's next chapter.

https://bit.ly/LanguageLoves

https://bit.ly/LovesLanguages

https://bit.ly/BalanceLifePlan

Here's the catch...

"He who fails to plan is planning to fail ." **Winston Churchill,** Take some time to plan by visiting the link below in this book section. Develop your plan!

https://yearcompass.com/

it's a free booklet, **but it may expire soon**. Helps you reflect on the year and plan for the next one. Learn from your mistakes, celebrate small victories, and set a path you want to walk on. Just a few hours and the booklet.

I T'S CRAZY; WITH ADVANCING communication outlets through social sites. Communication is at an all-time high— but not effective communication. We can't even hold a real conversation face-to-face. Communication is the bridge that connects two people. It's the art of building "every healthy" relationship we build, as Tony A. Gaskins Jr., life coach, said, "Without *it, it dies.*

So if your relationship is suffering, it could result from ineffective communication, but it's not your fault. We just model communicated the way we saw it growing up. Whether it was right or wrong. The good thing for you is that communication skills can be learned. In this book, we gave you very effective **strategies** and guided you through some of the steps we took and are still taking. This has allowed us to grow closer together and build a wonderful marriage for the past 17yrs and growing. If it's the Lord's will, we'll have many more years of happiness on earth. So take action with the new **strategies and** skills we've shared with you. Put god " daily " in your relationships, and get in a good community of people.

And, understand that when there's an inability to communicate effectively, there is a root cause. Then, you need to discover what the root cause is. Sometimes, it is as simple as controlling the childish version of an adult we adopted. Or you were just never taught how to communicate properly as a child like us.

The environment you were raised in may have modeled ineffective communication that included yelling, backbiting, avoiding, and silent treatments. You may have never seen your parents or caregivers communicate effectively. Maybe their relationships were nonexistent, just living together or whatever.

It may be unhealed trauma, a lack of trust, abandonment, unforgiveness, or fear caused by other reasons. For example, maybe the environment you grew up in was toxic and modeled abuse. Perhaps you were betrayed in a previous relationship (or friendship).

Whatever the case, you need to identify and work on the problem, capture it, release it, and move on. Get a Morning Ritual, work on spiritual and personal development, and work on yourself " daily ". Some people say to stay out of relationships until you are healed, and while this is partially good advice, we sometimes fail to remember that healing can be a lifelong journey. And you should not have to put your entire life on pause because of a few things you must heal from. Plus, healing is easier when you have a support system—which your partner could be for you.

This does not mean that your partner should be a crutch. And yes, you should heal before putting yourself in a situation to be hurt again. If not, you could risk engaging in unhealthy dating habits. The important thing to remember is to pace yourself. Your healing will take time. Forgiving yourself and those who caused your past pains will take some time. Getting to a point where you can look at the brighter side of things and accept what happened with an optimistic view of the future will take time. You have to control your emotions so they don't get the best of you.

And complete all of the steps in your process. You have to go through each phase. Some days will be more challenging than others, but what you don't want to do is get stuck. If you feel stuck on one phase for a while, " invest in yourself " and get help. A therapist, a trusted friend, a coach, a parent, or a partner are all people who can support you and encourage you on your journey. Just make sure they are wise in some form. Be honest with your partner about where you are and where you want to go.

Express your goals, feelings, and struggles and how you want to overcome them. Being transparent is scary, but it helps bring and keep you and your partner close through it all.

You don't want to neglect yourself, and you don't want to neglect your partner if you are working toward something better. Even while you are healing yourself, you and your partner can still benefit from your relationship. Take steps to make sure you're both taken care of. Set boundaries and be accountable for yourself by taking responsibility for your actions and words and owning up to your emotions. You can be the Powerful, or you can be connected. But you can't be both. When you step into the power, you lose the connection. Healthy relationships are built on connection; let your voice be heard. Just keep in mind you are a team, and there is no " I " in it. It's not about who's right or wrong. It's about how you can easily repair the conflict and return to loving your partner. We know you can do it! Have the 10-minute daily or weekly talk session, work toward forgiveness, and let the past be the past you, not the present you, and indeed not the future. Change your narrative. Instead of living victimized, choose to be an overcomer. We know you can do it!

We encourage you to read this book seven times to let it sink in. Then, if you choose, you both decide "both" of you will work to create a growing, healthy relationship. Then, write it down, take action daily, and you will begin to see the results of your recovery process.

More and more, you will be able to control your emotion. You'll be able to communicate better, rekindle intimacy, and improve your relationships.

You'll have a happy home with better sleep at night and change the communication in your family for the next generation because that's where it really counts!

Remember, You can be powerful, or connected, but you can be both.

Thank You; we hope this has helped you as much as it is helping us!

If You Received Value From This Book, Please Leave Us a 5-Star Review.

https://amzn.to/3L09kk3

You can help other couples find this book and gain the skills for effective communication and creating healthy relationships.

Get the vision, claim it, and go build a life together that you love...

A FREE GIFT TO OUR READERS

DEVELOPING INTIMATE RELATIONSHIPS THROUGH AUTHEN-TIC CONNECTION

https://bit.ly/Moreconnected

While It Lasts!

How To Connect With Us

youtube.com/@TNL.Jrelationshipcoaches

facebook.com/TonyaNLamont

Relationship Coaching Program Coming Soon. Connect With Us On Our Website Below!

https://www.tonyanlamontonline.com/

Here's The Link For All the Worksheets And Workbooks On One Page

https://bit.ly/TandLBonusWorkbook

References

Acosta, J. (2021, April 2). *Healing old wounds — Letting go in 6 steps*. Invisible Illness. https://medium.com/invisible-illness/healing-old-wounds-letting-go-in-6-steps-ec5915703144

Agha, W. (2019, October 10). *What is mosting and why is it even worse than ghosting?* BingeCulture. https://www.bingedaily.in/article/what-is-mosting-and-why-is-it-even-worse-than-ghosting

Alpert, J. (2015, November 3). *7 tips for saying no effectively*. Inc.com. https://www.inc.com/jonathan-alpert/7-ways-to-say-no-to-someone-and-not-feel-bad-about-it.html

Altschule, S. (2014, October 27). *How to keep your relationship alive*. Bustle. https://www.bustle.com/articles/45366-10-habits-of-couples-in-strong-and-healthy-relationships

Altschule, S. (2016, February 5). *7 things that can have a major impact on your romantic relationships*. Bustle. https://www.bustle.com/articles/139139-7-things-that-can-have-a-major-impact-on-your-romantic-relationship

Andrade, S. (2021, June 1). *The importance of setting healthy boundaries*. Forbes.

https://www.forbes.com/sites/forbescoachescouncil/2021/07/01/the-importance-of-setting-healthy-boundaries/?sh=babaa1456e46

Beauchamp, M. (2022, August 10). *What is gaslighting in a relationship?* Brides. https://www.brides.com/gaslighting-in-relationships-5112026

Beauchamp, M. (2022, August 16). *What is breadcrumbing? A relationship expert explains.* Brides. https://www.brides.com/what-is-breadcrumbing-5105353

Beck, M. (n.d.). *The key to healing emotional wounds.* Oprah.com. Retrieved October 23, 2022, from

1 Corinthians 13:11 When I was a child, I talked like a child, I ....

Bennett, T. (2022, March 10). *Trust issues: Signs, causes, and how to overcome them.* Thriveworks.com. https://thriveworks.com/blog/trust-issues/

Benwell, M. (2018, March 1). *Ghosting, caspering, and six new dating terms you've never heard of.* The Guardian. https://www.theguardian.com/lifeandstyle/2018/feb/28/six-new-dating-terms-youve-never-heard-of

Better health channel. (2022, February 24). *Strong relationships, strong health.* Vic.gov.au. https://www.betterhealth.vic.gov.au/health/HealthyLiving/Strong-relationships-strong-health

Borges, A. (2020, May 18). *17 totally normal things to experience in your relationship right now.* SELF. https://www.self.com/story/pandemic-relationship-problems

Boundaries are so important in recovery. (2019, February 21). Ashley Addiction Treatment. https://www.ashleytreatment.org/boundaries-in-recovery/

Brenner, H. (2017). *6 ways that a rough childhood can affect adult relationships.* Psychology Today. https://www.psychologytoday.com/us/blog/experimentations/201707/6-ways-rough-childhood-can-affect-adult-relationships

Brickel, R. (2016, April 28). *Loving a trauma survivor: Understanding childhood trauma's impact on relationships.* PsychAlive. https://www.psychalive.org/loving-trauma-survivor-understanding-childhood-traumas-impact-relationships/

Brown, J. (2022, October 12). *Micro-cheating sounds innocent. And it is. Until it isn't.* Fatherly. https://www.fatherly.com/love-money/what-is-micro-cheating-and-is-it-ruining-your-marriage

Calloway, M. N.-P. (2020, February 12). *Ghosting vs. caspering: How to let them down easy.* Northwest Public Broadcasting. https://www.nwpb.org/2020/02/12/ghosting-vs-caspering-how-to-let-them-down-easy/

Chaterjee, D. (2020, September 21). *What is ghosting in a relationship? Here's how it affects people.* PINKVILLA. https://www.pinkvilla.com/lifestyle/love-relationships/what-ghosting-relationship-here-s-how-it-affects-people-563795

Cherry, K. (2022, January 18). *Why you may have trust issues and how to overcome them.* Verywell Mind. https://www.verywellmind.com/why-you-may-have-trust-issues-and-how-to-overcome-them-5215390

Chesak, J. (2018, December 10). *The no BS guide to setting healthy boundaries in real life.* Healthline. https://www.healthline.com/health/mental-health/set-boundaries#how-to-communicate-and-set-your-boundaries

Chuckdisaccount. (2021, December 3). *Poor communication is destroying my relationship.* Reddit. https://www.reddit.com/r/relationships/comments/r7li0q/poor_communication_is_destroying_my_relationship/

Cliff, M. (2020, November 18). The *secret signs your bloke's a cheat & why "peacocking" is the biggest tell of all.* The Sun. https://www.thesun.co.uk/fabulous/13225788/secret-signs-man-cheating-on-you/

Conti, G. (2020, May 12). *Zombie-ing is the scary Coronavirus dating trend you literally didn't ask for.* Cosmopolitan. https://www.cosmopol itan.com/sex-love/a29210551/zombieing-dating-definition/

Deloe, J. (2016, June 10). *15 common signs of unresolved trauma.* Healthy Place. https://www.healthyplace.com/blogs/traumaptsdblog/2016/0 6/15-common-signs-of-unresolved-trauma

Dowling, D. (n.d.). *A 10-minute ritual to improve communication in your relationship.* The Daily Positive. Retrieved October 23, 2022, from https://www.thedailypositive.com/10-minute-ritual-improve-c ommunication-in-your-relationship/

Dubin, M. (2022, February 14). *Dating, ghosting, mosting, and more.* Georgia Voice - Gay & LGBT Atlanta News. https://thegavoice.com/o utspoken/dating-ghosting-mosting-and-more/

Earlam, S. (2010). *How does communication affect the quality of close relationships?* Counseling Directory. https://www.counselling-directory.org.uk/memberarticles/how -does-communication-affect-the-quality-of-close-relationships

Earnshaw, E. (2014, June 12). *How lack of communication sneakily ruins relationships.* Mindbodygreen. https://www.mindbodygreen.com/0-1 4106/5-communication-mistakes-that-kill-relationships.html

Editorial Contributors. (2021, October 25). *Setting boundaries.* Web-MD. https://www.webmd.com/mental-health/setting-boundaries

Editorial Contributors. (2020, November 17). *Signs of trust issues.* WebMD. https://www.webmd.com/mental-health/signs-trust-issues

Editors of Men's Health. (2018, November 13). *Sharting while naked, and other crazy relationship stories from Reddit.* Men's Health. https://www.menshealth.com/sex-women/a25046715/crazy -reddit-relationship-stories/

Ellefsen, C. (2013, November 22). *The art of forgiveness.* The Art of Simple. https://www.theartofsimple.net/debt-cavities-art-and-forgi veness/

Estrada, J. (2020, January 4). *How to rebuild trust in a relationship after the damage has been done*. Well+Good. https://www.wellandgood.com/how-to-rebuild-trust/

Fabello, M. (2020, September 13). *So you're a ghost guy, like-to-disappear guy*. Greatist. https://greatist.com/connect/science-of-ghosting

5 reasons why learning to say no is an important life skill. (2017, June 22). Nandyz Soulshine. https://nandyzsoulshine.com/saying-no-important-life-skill/

Five ways to say "no" without being rude. (2014, September 2). The Economic Times. https://economictimes.indiatimes.com/work-career/five-ways-to-say-no-without-being-rude/slideshow/41479384.cms

Flinn, A. (2020, May 13). *I'm a couples therapist, and these are the 6 biggest communication issues I see in relationships*. Well+Good. https://www.wellandgood.com/communication-issues-in-relationships/

Freer, B. (2019, April 15). *What to do if physical intimacy disappears from your relationship*? The Awareness Centre. https://theawarenesscentre.com/physical-intimacy-disappears-from-relationship

Garbaggiojones. (2019, May 8). *Catch and release*. Reddit. https://www.reddit.com/r/datingoverthirty/comments/bm6y0c/catch_and_release/

Gaspard, T. (2016, December 8). *10 ways to rekindle the passion in your marriage*. The Gottman Institute. https://www.gottman.com/blog/10-ways-rekindle-passion-marriage/

Goodman, J., Pugachevsky, J., & Evans, M. (2019, February 11). *Here's how to know if you're micro-cheating*. Cosmopolitan. https://www.cosmopolitan.com/sex-love/a18930027/how-to-tell-if-youre-micro-cheating/

Griffin, T. (2021, April 14). *How to forgive someone who betrays you*. WikiHow. https://www.wikihow.com/Forgive-Someone-Who-Betrays-You

Habib, S. (2019, October 15). *Stories of effective communication.* Lifecl ub.org. https://lifeclub.org/p/effective-communication

Hayes, A. (2019, July 4). *You're probably peacocking without even realizing it. Here's what it means.* Men's Health. https://www.menshealth.co m/uk/sex/a28257576/peacocking/

His friend circle is the problem. (2018, October 1). The Times of India. https://timesofindia.indiatimes.com/life-style/relationships/love-sex /7-married-couples-talk-about-external-factors-that-damage-their-r elationship/photostory/66028703.cms?picid=66028816

How good communication leads to greater intimacy in marriage. (2015, February 6). The Humbled Homemaker. https://thehumbledhomema ker.com/marriage-communication/

How to fix a relationship that lacks intimacy and connection. (2018, August 4). A Conscious Rethink. https://www.aconsciousrethink.com/8 484/relationship-lacks-intimacy-connection/

Jiang, K. (2021, January 28). *Emotional intimacy: 12 ways to get and give more of it.* Greatist. https://greatist.com/connect/emotional-intimacy #how-to-built-it

Johnson, E. B. (2020a, January 14). *Get out of the zombie zone to get into a fulfilling relationship.* Practical Growth. https://medium.com/practical-growth/get-out-of-the-zom bie-zone-for-better-relationships-e00cce917b86

Johnson, E. B. (2020b, September 25). *How to forgive someone after a major betrayal.* Practical Growth. https://medium.com/practical-grow th/how-to-forgive-someone-after-a-betrayal-6db52a9bbbea

Kassel, G. (2019, November 25). *Is "micro-cheating" actually an issue?* Healthline. https://www.healthline.com/health/micro-cheating

Kogan, V. (2021, March 22). *Council Post: The art of forgiveness: A key to high-performance leadership.* Forbes. https://www.forbes.com/sites/forbescoachescouncil/2021/03/22/the

-art-of-forgiveness-a-key-to-high-performance-leadership/?sh=1102 67573ff3

Kozlowski, T. (2019, August 13). *Why personal boundaries are important and how to set them.* TerryKozlowski.com. *https://terrikozlowski.co m/why-personal-boundaries-are-important-and-how-to-set-them/*

Laderer, A. (2022, March 21). *If someone keeps giving you hope that they'll commit but never does, you might be getting breadcrumbed.* Insider. https://www.insider.com/guides/health/sex-relationships/breadc rumbing

Laderer, A. (2022, October 19). *How to spot gaslighting: 6 things that gaslighters say to manipulate you.* Insider. https://www.insider.com/gu ides/health/sex-relationships/gaslighting-examples

Lamothe, C. (2019, October 29). *Lack of communication: 17 tips for couples.* Healthline. https://www.healthline.com/health/lack-of-com munication#signs-of-a-problem

Lebow, H. (2021, June 10). *Do your early experiences affect your adult relationships?* Psych Central. https://psychcentral.com/blog/how-chil dhood-trauma-affects-adult-relationships

Leinwand, L. (2016, November 10). *Why is saying "no" so important?* GoodTherapy. https://www.goodtherapy.org/blog/why-is-saying-no -so-important-1110165

Loggins, B. (2022, October 19). *What is breadcrumbing?* Verywell Mind. https://www.verywellmind.com/what-is-breadcrumbing-522 0677

Loggins, B. (2021, November 23). *Childhood trauma in adults: How to recognize and heal from it.* Verywell Mind. https://www.verywellmind. com/signs-of-childhood-trauma-in-adults-5207979

Lutin, N. (2014, September 23). *How to say "no" without being rude. 5 ways!* MyTherapyNYC. https://mytherapynyc.com/say-without-rude/

Martin, S. (2019, March 22). *8 tips for healing emotional wounds.* Psych Cen-

tral. https://psychcentral.com/blog/imperfect/2019/03/8-tips-for-he
aling-emotional-wounds#Tips-for-healing-from-emotional-wounds

Martin, S. (2017, March 5). *Benefits of setting boundaries: Why you need
to set healthy boundaries.* Live Well with Sharon Martin. https://www.l
ivewellwithsharonmartin.com/6-benefits-of-setting-boundaries/

McElhenney, J. (2018, May 21). *Dating lessons: Gentle catch and release.*
The Whole Parent. https://wholeparentbook.com/dating-lessons-gen
tle-catch-and-release/

Mental   Health   Foundation.   (2016,   May   15).   *Relationships   in   the   21st   century: The   forgotten   foundation   of
mental   health   and   wellbeing.*   Mental   Health   Foundation. https://www.mentalhealth.org.uk/publications/relationships-2
1st-century-forgotten-foundation-mental-health-and-wellbeing

Narrow-Home7759. (2022, April 27). *Trust issues and it's affecting my
current relationship.* Reddit. https://www.reddit.com/r/trustissues/co
mments/ud7l30/trust_issues_and_its_affecting_my_current/

Nelson, T. (2019, December 18). *The 3 phases of erotic recovery after
infidelity.* Recovery.org. https://recovery.org/pro/articles/the-3-phase
s-of-erotic-recovery-after-infidelity/

Nelson, S. (2015, July 9). *The art of forgiveness: 5 things you need to know.*
Sivana East. https://blog.sivanaspirit.com/why-you-should-forgive/

9 terms that define modern dating. (2018, May 25). Business Insider.
https://www.businessinsider.in/slideshows/miscellaneous/9-terms-t
hat-define-modern-dating/slidelist/64322562.cms#slideid=64322563

Pace, R. (2019, May 13). *What are the effects of a lack of communication
in a relationship?* Marriage. https://www.marriage.com/advice/comm
unication/no-communication-in-a-relationship/

Pattemore, C. (2021, June 3). *10 ways to build and preserve better boundaries.* Psych Central. https://psychcentral.com/lib/10-way-to-build-a
nd-preserve-better-boundaries

Paul, M. (2012, December 14). *7 ingredients of a healthy relationship: Is your relationship healthy?* HuffPost. https://www.huffpost.com/entry/relationship-advice_b_2270527

Pommerenk, D. A. (2019, September 16). *Accountability in relationships begins in the first moment you engage.* Mind Cafe. https://medium.com/mind-cafe/accountability-in-relationship-begins-in-the-first-moment-you-engage-e9b2dbc21d22

Popescu, A. (2019, January 22). *Why people ghost—and how to get over it.* The New York Times. https://www.nytimes.com/2019/01/22/smarter-living/why-people-ghost-and-how-to-get-over-it.html

Pugachevsky, J. (2019, July 29). *How to tell if your date is totally peacocking.* Cosmopolitan. https://www.cosmopolitan.com/sex-love/a28540112/peacocking-meaning-definition/

Raypole, C. (2019, August 9). *How to rebuild trust after a betrayal.* Healthline Media. https://www.healthline.com/health/how-to-rebuild-trust

Saint Thomas, S. (2019, July 17). *Caspering is a new dating trend that's actually worse than ghosting.* Allure. https://www.allure.com/story/caspering-new-dating-trend-ghosting

Sangerma, E. (2021, January 20). *6 signs your relationship has real communication issues.* Medium. https://medium.com/wholistique/6-signs-your-relationship-has-real-communication-issues-2034c33ebd9

7 steps to understanding the importance of communication in a relationship. (2019, February 26). OurRelationship. https://www.ourrelationship.com/7-steps-to-understanding-the-importance-of-communication-in-a-relationship/

Shah, J. (n.d.). *Sexual communication - Why is it important for couples?.* Lybrate. Retrieved October 23, 2022, from https://www.lybrate.com/topic/sexual-communication-why-is-it-important-for-couples/0b69830a502b8418b5c6a9807ac9c752

Signs you may be dealing with lingering effects of childhood trauma. (n.d.). Institute for Advanced Psychiatry. https://www.psychiatryfortworth.com/blog/signs-you-may-be-dealing-with-lingering-effects-of-childhood-trauma

Smith, S. (2021, June 23). *The importance of communication in relationships.* Marriage. https://www.marriage.com/advice/communication/importance-of-communication-in-relationships/

Stahl, A. (2015, October 2). *Three reasons you need to say "no" more often.* Forbes. https://www.forbes.com/sites/ashleystahl/2015/10/02/three-reasons-you-need-to-say-no-more-often/?sh=163e501e3ff3

Stern, R. (2018, December 19). *Gaslighting in relationships: How to spot it and shut it down.* Vox. https://www.vox.com/first-person/2018/12/19/18140830/gaslighting-relationships-politics-explained

Stosny, S. (2019, May 22). *Intimacy and communication.* Psychology Today. https://www.psychologytoday.com/us/blog/anger-in-the-age-entitlement/201905/intimacy-and-communication

Streep, P. (2019, August 9). *12 signs of healing from a toxic childhood.* Psychology Today. https://www.psychologytoday.com/us/blog/tech-support/201908/12-signs-healing-toxic-childhood

Stritof, S. (2003, December 14). *Forgiveness and letting go in your marriage.* Verywell Mind. https://www.verywellmind.com/forgiveness-and-letting-go-in-marriage-2300611

Swift, J. (2017, December 6). *The influence of relationships.* Cornell Research. https://research.cornell.edu/news-features/influence-relationships

Umberson, D., & Karas Montez, J. (2010). Social relationships and health: A flashpoint for health policy. *Journal of Health and Social Behavior, 51*(suppl), S54–S66.

Proverbs 4:7-9 - Bible.

https://yearcompass.com/ Your Year Compass | The booklet that helps close your year and plan the next one..

Kirsten Nunez (Feb 21, 2020) https://www.healthline.com/health/ment al-health/fight-flight-freeze#overactive-response

https://www.therapyroute.com/article/heartful-listening-the-feedback-w heel-communication-techniques-by-s-carter

Made in United States
Troutdale, OR
07/21/2023

11441165R30126